A
VIEW
FROM
THE ACADEMY

Liberal Arts Professors
on Excellent Teaching

Thomas Warren, Editor
Beloit College

Association of
Independent Liberal Arts Colleges
for Teacher Education
and University Press of America

UNIVERSITY
PRESS OF
AMERICA

Lanham • New York • London

Copyright © 1992 by
University Press of America®, Inc.
4720 Boston Way
Lanham, Maryland 20706

3 Henrietta Street
London WC2E 8LU England

Co-published by arrangement with the
Association of Independent Liberal Arts Colleges
for Teacher Education

Library of Congress Cataloging-in-Publication Data

A view from the academy : liberal arts professors on excellent
teaching / Thomas Warren, editor.
p.   cm.
1. College teaching—United States.   2. Education, Humanistic—
United States.   I. Warren, Thomas, 1939–
LB2331.V54   1992   378.1'25'0973—dc20   92–11629 CIP

ISBN 0–8191–8667–8 (cloth : alk. paper)
ISBN 0–8191–8668–6 (pbk. : alk. paper)

Contents

Foreword

The Association of Independent Liberal Arts Colleges for Teacher Education (AILACTE) is delighted to continue its monograph series with this second volume, *A View from the Academy: Liberal Arts Professors on Excellent Teaching.* The first monograph in the series, *A View from the Top: Liberal Arts Presidents on Teacher Education,* presented the perspectives of liberal arts college presidents on teacher education. *A View from the Academy* shares what our liberal arts colleagues believe about their own teaching and the role of teaching in their institutions.

The decade of the 1990s brings increased interest in teaching from many directions. Concern about the quality of teaching in public schools and universities is high. In 1988 the American Council on Education published *Turning Professors into Teachers,* the results of two projects conducted between 1978 and 1987 involving fifteen institutions. It was supported by the Fund for the Improvement of Postsecondary Education (FIPSE) and the Ford Foundation. The authors, Joseph Katz and Mildred Henry, conclude that "the force of teaching resides in its individualizing effect on the student and begins with the development of the teacher's individuality . . . [that] deepens one's knowledge of oneself as a professional and as a person and [that] can generate a fresh and enduring enthusiasm for teaching. Such discovery allows teachers to help their students make their own discoveries" (p. 5). Katz and Henry believe that "teachers become practitioners and investigators at the same time."

Ernest Boyer promotes a similar notion in *Scholarship Reconsidered* (1990). He documents that scholarship in American higher education has moved through three distinct phases: (1) a focus on building character and intellect, preparing colonial students for civic and religious leadership; (2) a shift of focus to the building of a nation with its emphasis on the practical side of higher learning and adding service as a mission to land grant institutions; and (3) during the last century with the rise of the scientific method, a shift of emphasis to the advancement of knowledge through research.

Boyer believes that if America's colleges and universities are to remain vital, scholarship must be reconsidered, and he sees four overlapping functions of the professoriate that can nurture this vitality. He calls them the scholarship of discovery, the scholarship of integration, the scholarship of application, and the scholarship of teaching. He agrees with Aristotle that good teaching is not only transmitting knowledge, but transforming and extending it as well.

Liberal arts colleges promote themselves as institutions that teach students to integrate and apply knowledge. Arts and science colleagues who teach at such places view themselves as teachers first. In AILACTE institutions the link between us and them is strong as we prepare teachers who are well-educated and who can well-teach.

Our association salutes exemplary teaching and thoughtful consideration of teaching by arts and sciences colleagues at AILACTE institutions across the country. In this second monograph we present with pride some of these colleagues' views of their own teaching. We are glad that they wave the banner for teaching with those of us who are more obviously a part of teacher education. Thank you, contributors, for sharing your expertise and thoughts.

Earline Kendall
President, AILACTE
1992–1993

Preface
Excellent Teachers in Our Midst

Clearly, liberal arts colleges value excellent teaching. This is not to say that they have a monopoly on it or that other types of educational institutions diminish its importance. The fact is that virtually all colleges and universities of the type that make up the membership of the Association of Independent Liberal Arts Colleges for Teacher Education (AILACTE) take teaching seriously and justifiably have pride in what happens in their classrooms.

Furthermore, teaching about excellent teaching is a high priority of every Department of Education within AILACTE institutions. These efforts have a set of potential partners nearby in the excellent teachers who are colleagues in other departments on campus. Whenever a faculty member of any department demonstrates effective teaching, it furthers the teacher education efforts of the institution, because students who are future teachers need to experience good teaching wherever it may be. The more the better. The more innovative and varied styles of excellence, the better. The more places it is found, the better.

While the foregoing brand of comments elicits few arguments and considerable support from teacher educators, interdisciplinary communication in our institutions is not as far along as it could be. All teacher education programs do not as a matter of course acknowledge or take good advantage of the pool of effective teachers that is near them in other departments. With the goal of promoting better sharing of our institutional talents and insights, this monograph introduces readers to some of the excellent teachers who are in our midst.

A View from the Academy: Liberal Arts Professors on Excellent Teaching picks up on a theme from AILACTE's first monograph, *A View from the Top: Liberal Arts Presidents on Teacher Education,* by stressing that wide institutional support and collegiality are necessary for teacher education programs to flourish. This second book consists of twenty original articles written by twenty-one authors.* They were chosen from a pool of nominees put forth by teacher educators from the Association. A selection committee narrowed them down to a smaller number that were invited to submit manuscripts.

The invitation to participate included the following statements:

"... Recognizing the fact that teacher education is a multi-disciplinary effort and that excellent teaching is a campus-wide priority of AILACTE colleges and universities, this second monograph of the Association will consist of a collection of articles by non-Education faculty members who are acknowledged to be excellent teachers. They will write articles focusing on the dual themes of: (1) what is behind their own effectiveness as teachers and (2) the role of first-rate teaching in liberal arts colleges.

"... You and your fellow authors will be given wide latitude to comment on your teaching successes. For example, you may address your philosophies of learning, subject matter expertise, teaching styles, scholarly pursuits, interaction with the world outside of the college, enthusiasm, relationships to students, co-operative efforts, "How I learn from experience," "How I learn from students," and/or other ways that help readers learn about your teaching.

"... As a contributor you must also comment on the broader issue of how you understand the role of quality teaching in higher education. For example, what should be the place of quality teaching relative to scholarship

---

* One article is co-authored by two faculty members from Pacific Lutheran University.

for undergraduates? What is the role of college teaching excellence in the education of kindergarten to twelfth grade teachers? How can administrations and colleagues support high quality teaching in college?"

Every one of the twenty-one authors selected agreed to participate. One invitee, Fred Oscanyan, died before he could respond, and we are saddened by the lost opportunity to learn about his teaching. Professor Oscanyan was a member of the Department of Philosophy at Berea College in Kentucky. His distinguished academic career included participation in the development and expansion of the Philosophy for Children program in Kentucky and a course in Philosophy for Children at Berea that is recommended for education students.

Of the twenty-one authors, five each are from the disciplines of English and History. Biology has two contributors as do Religion and Philosophy when Professor Kasulis is represented in both categories. Anthropology, Communications/ Theatre Arts, Mathematics/Computer science, Physics/ Astronomy, and Sociology have one author each. In terms of broader academic divisions, the natural sciences contributed four articles, the social sciences (including History) and humanities eight each.

Geographically, institutions from fourteen states are represented. Wisconsin has five contributors; Iowa, Massachusetts, Ohio, and Tennessee each have two; and Colorado, Indiana, Kentucky, New Jersey, New York, North Carolina, South Carolina, Texas, and Washington have one each.

Many people helped to write this volume. The authors deserve the most credit. Without their ready willingness to devote creativity, time, and energy, it would not have turned out to be so informative and comprehensive. The membership and Executive Committee of AILACTE have been supportive from the start. They asked good questions and provided ideas at several points along the way. An editorial committee consisting of Phil Bennett of Mid-America Nazarene College, Earline Kendall of Belmont College, and Charlotte Mendoza of Colorado College read every manuscript and worked with me to standardize and sharpen them as needed. "Gentle editing" was our approach since care and attention to detail characterized the manuscripts sent by the authors. At the many campuses where articles and editorial comments were typed and corrected are secretaries and others who assisted in many ways. David Heesen, Head of the Beloit College Secretarial Services, deserves a special thanks for his many talents and cheerful willingness to help.

Thomas Warren
Beloit College
Publications Editor, AILACTE

Introduction

Prof. Laura Winters says it simply: "There is nothing more important in the formulation of excellent teachers than excellent teaching." This second monograph of the Association of Independent Liberal Arts Colleges for Teacher Education (AILACTE) features original articles by twenty-one college teachers all of whom are acknowledged to be excellent in the classroom. They write about their own effectiveness and the role of quality teaching in liberal arts settings. The articles themselves are unique in style and substance, but certain themes cut across virtually every presentation, and they all project an enthusiasm for and dedication to teaching. While the authors regularly are called "professor" with its various connotations, they acknowledge that nothing they do is more important than teaching, and they proudly answer to the title of "teacher."

Teaching is more of an art than a science to these people. Their individuality and that of their students comes across loud and clear. They see "getting through" to students as a first priority of their work. In addressing this task they realize that students must be active partners and that they, the teachers, influence whether and how students participate.

Several authors refer to "conversation" and the various "voices" that participate in it. Patricia O'Connell Killen and Dennis Martin, co-authors of the article "Learning as Conversation" note that ". . . [T]he context for genuine conversation will have a different tone, texture, and subject content depending on the course, students, and instructors, [but there are] characteristics of such classroom contexts which . . . are identifiable across disciplinary lines."

Marcia Ann McDonald says that her primary metaphor for teaching is conversation. "My goal is to enable my students to

1

join the conversation and recognize patterns that conversation takes." While such a conception of the teacher-student role may be strange and unfamiliar to students (and many teachers), McDonald would rather take risks with a format that some students resist than ". . . settle for secure patterns that may make students too comfortable with their college education."

John Oppelt judges his effectiveness as a teacher on whether he can maintain a good conversation which he describes as ". . . content, a common vocabulary, sensitive listening, clarity of expression, asking questions without presuming answers, and a respect for those with whom I am conversing." Knowledge of subject matter is utterly important to such a relationship. It happens when teachers really know something well. If teachers are not on top of what the conversation entails, success is unlikely. Oppelt confides that, "When I teach in a subject that is close to the edge of my knowledge, the classroom conversation disappears."

Students who participate in class conversations are unique individuals with various things to contribute according to Donna Bauerly in her article called "The Many Voices of the Classroom." Her goal is to help students be heard in all their candor and individuality. This job is not just the teachers', however. Students must be active learners as well.

No contributor to this volume assumes that students can learn effectively if they are passive and dependent. Students must assert themselves while their teachers offer opportunities and provide leadership, at least for a while. William Wooley puts it like this: ". . . the overarching goal of all undergraduate education is . . . the liberation of the maturing individual from a state of dependence to a state of independence . . ." and students must learn that the key to responding lies with themselves rather than within any given orthodoxy. Students must become thinking, discerning individuals, and their teachers help the development through establishing an academic relationship with them. Janet Griffen comments that all the learning methods in the world cannot be effective unless there is a good relationship between the teacher and the student, and Timothy Garner reminds us that we must teach

2

with the assumption that the intellectual self does not exist in a relational vacuum.

However, relationships do not occur automatically. Sometimes the particular mix of students in a class is enough to ignite dynamic exchanges, and as Thomas Kasulis points out, the teacher should make sure that positive relationships happen. "As the teacher I am responsible for how the group relates to each other," he says. "Do I effectively direct the rhythms of the class, going back and forth between the general and the specific, the humorous and the serious, the technical and the practical?"

Back to the matter of students as active learners: Establishing relationships among them and between them and the teacher requires that the teacher is not the sole decision-maker in the class. Bruce Griffith refers to Pericles who says that Athens was wiser than her rivals because all of her citizens participated in the process of decision-making. Similarly, as Garner puts it, the fact that an individual student gains a sense of ownership with respect to the class helps that student develop a sense of self. Her or his opinion matters, and it can have an impact on others.

Harvey Klevar in his autobiographical article warns us that power is involved in the relationship between teacher and student and when students actively participate in decision-making, the power of the teacher can be threatened, but this does not seem to be a major obstacle to some of our authors including Klevar. Winters reflects that "Love is the refusal to think of another person in terms of power" and then adds "I often call upon that definition when dealing with my students in and out of the classroom." Frances Chew calls the giving up of control as exhilarating. Others describe how they share power. Rose Marie Hurrell says, "When a change in the details of my course syllabus is called for, I negotiate with students to avoid hardship or unpleasant surprises." Klevar shares how he allows student to influence their grades on a given assignment. "Grades are not carved in stone. The work can be revised and grades raised."

Astronomer Dan Schroeder provides opportunities for pairs of students to observe the sky with separate telescopes in order to encourage a pool of unique perspectives. When students come up with an "answer" that he may not necessarily want to endorse, he reminds himself, "They're not dumb; they're different." Schroeder and Mary Ball agree that the best student insights do not necessarily come right away; but when the [spoken or unspoken] shout of "Eureka," "Aha," or "Oh, I see now" emerges, teaching and learning are at their best.

Just as teachers may be intimidated by or reluctant to share decision-making, students often gingerly enter academic dialogue. Joseph Buckley observes, "The place where we [the teachers] and they [the students] meet is where they are . . . and they are scared." Buckley tries to help the meeting by not taking himself too seriously and by welcoming the students into his circle. "Hello, philosophers!" is his greeting.

Jesse Scott says ". . . good teachers treat students like people. Students have names and faces, and they should deserve respect." Similarly, Chew sees peer interaction as critical for a successful classroom and as the norm in scientific research. She strives to teach collaborative skills and is convinced that peer interaction helps learners take charge. Lucy Cromwell tries to concentrate on what her students are doing rather than herself. Hurrell sees learning partnership as the very essence of teaching: ". . . [T]o teach is to participate as a partner in learning." Truth itself is interactive according to Killen and Martin. Both teachers and students benefit from the exchange.

Student-oriented education has its ostensible drawbacks, and it is unrealistic to think that all teachers will readily move away from the protection of their podiums. Wooley acknowledges the amount of time that is consumed and the coherence that is sometimes strained when a learning partnership between teacher and students is attempted. He may agree with Scott's characterization: "Teaching is the equivalent of whitewater rafting. All teachers sooner or later capsize, and they regularly ask themselves whether they are doing the right thing."

Our twenty-one authors do not subscribe to a single teaching style or a prescribed set of styles. They all at least implicitly support a variety of approaches and attest to the help they get from their colleagues. Unfortunately, too many teachers at all

4

levels work alone with minimal collaboration with their peers. This problem and its solution are addressed by a number of our authors. Kasulis gets to the heart of the matter when he writes, "I suspect that the best way to make teachers better is to get them to talk with each other about teaching." Many others agree.

Winters says, "Good teachers never work alone. They may sometimes work in opposition to systems which don't value their contributions, but to be an excellent teacher one must have a community of like-minded people, no matter how small or geographically distant." Oppelt articulates one of the key reasons behind the development of this monograph when he says ". . . the education and training of preservice teachers can and should become the responsibility of the entire faculty." In order for that goal to be realized, they must communicate with each other.

While communication involves faculty members learning from one another, an institution's administration can play an important role in setting the tone, a point articulated by Griffin who commends her administration for sponsoring a "Faculty Idea Exchange." One can readily see that a number of other authors also work in settings that are conducive to interchange of ideas. Killen and Martin say, "We teach at a university in which teaching excellence is valued." David Oswald adds, "I work at an institution where quality teaching is valued as the first priority. Colleagues talk on a regular, if not daily basis [about teaching].

Griffith shares the fact that his colleagues have helped him and that collaboration is an effective technique for promoting student learning, but it happens too infrequently and ". . . the egos of faculty are bruised in the frankly critical nature of our collaboration." Dialogue with fellow teachers whose style is radically different from his has helped Griffith understand students who are unlike him.

Robert McJimsey says that cooperative teaching attests to the versatility of liberal learning. "Every year I (an historian) teach with at least two colleagues usually in political science, English literature, or art history. Few if any subjects are impervious to a shared format." He also says that liberal learning honors versatility by offering students a variety of subjects and by giving each student a generous latitude of choice. Liberal learning remains skeptical of dogma, absolutes, and specialization. Excellent teaching involves an appreciation for the heritage of liberal learning and the mastery of pedagogy appropriate to the transmission of that heritage. McJimsey admits that his own teaching has evolved from stand-up lectures, to a mixture of lectures and recitation, to his present *modus operandi* where students take the lead.

Buckley's thoughts complement McJimsey's. Buckley submits that the liberal arts themselves have an advantage in promoting learning and that the focus of liberal arts teaching addresses the emotional and moral concerns of students as well as their intellectual lives.

Metaphors abound as our contributors share what has worked for them in the classroom or what they understand as the essence of teaching. Ball sees the teacher as a "fellow traveler," someone who points the way for others who ask direction but who learns for oneself in the process. Killen and Martin refer to their in-class collaboration as "doubles tennis" where both partners are in play all the time with roles changing in reaction to the situation. "Team teaching provides the opportunity to teach in slow motion," they say. "We cannot both speak at the same time. This makes us more careful about what we will say."

McDonald's students need "road maps" and "compasses" which she can provide, but the final destination must be their own. McJimsey uses the eighteenth century's "salon" and "literary club" to turn his classes into models of informed conversations. Cromwell says her classroom is "an arena" in which students can learn.

Schroeder uses metaphors in his teaching of physics and astronomy to define a scale factor which reduces the distance from the Earth to the sun to only 20 feet.

> [In this model] the sun is about the size of an orange and the Earth is the size of the tip of a ballpoint pen. The moon in this model is a speck of dust about one-half inch from the Earth and is the distance humankind has traveled into the vast universe! In this same model the most distant planet, Pluto, is 800 feet from the sun and the nearest star is about 1000 miles from earth. Another

way to illustrate the immensity of these distances is to assume a spaceship traveling at 100,000 miles per hour. At this rate it takes a little over two hours to reach the moon, nearly five years to reach Pluto, and about 30,000 years to get to the nearest star!"

Schroeder uses examples such as these to bring otherwise incomprehensible distances into a range which students can begin to understand. In the very small world of physics and the very large world of astronomy, they are valuable tools.

Historian Wooley, like virtually all of our authors, aims at relating his subject matter to the students' frames of reference. "I design my courses to be a set of experiences rather than packages of knowledge." Hurrell, a psychologist, confides that she is unable to disguise or hide her emotions so she uses them to fuel and humanize her teaching. She also sometimes elicits responses from students by asking questions such as "What color was your adolescence?"

Several of our contributors refer to excellent teachers that have influenced them. Winters says "We all must consciously imagine and create narratives of our lives, and the teachers we remember best remind us of that fact." Scott remains indebted to a college teacher who still influences him. "Professor McKale did not dwell on our inadequacies and . . . youthful ignorance. Instead he showed us our capabilities and potentialities . . ." Scott remembers back to the end of the last class of a course taught by this person: ". . . suddenly all thirty or so students began to applaud."

Teacher educators regularly bemoan the fact that their students are tempted to teach as they were taught, a practice that does not necessarily open them up to a wide cross-section of possibilities. Of course if the future teachers' teachers embodied excellence, then there would be little concern with teaching as one was taught. Bauerly apparently had fine role models. ". . . I teach as I was taught," she says. "Hopefully, so will my students."

The task of educating teachers would be so much easier if all of their own past and present teachers were worthy of emulations. Humbly but not hesitatingly this volume submits that liberal arts colleges value teaching emphatically, and that the teaching which occurs in these institutions plays a major role in addition to education classes in the making of teachers.

In fact teaching excellence in all college subjects is critical to sending out a teaching force that invigorates American classrooms. When the ideas and practices discussed and presented in education classes are reinforced in other classes at a college, the whole teacher education enterprise gains; when one-dimensional, professor-centered, doctrinaire teaching forges on and makes up a substantial part of a student's general education experience, something is missing and inconsistent.

Griffith states the dilemma like this: "It must be very confusing for our future teachers to learn that certain methodologies are essential to good teaching and then in the next period, to observe a professor who violates virtually all of those methodological principles." Similarly, Oppelt says, "If the teacher education that preservice students receive in their professional courses is in conflict with the experience they receive in content courses, how can we expect the students to mesh the two?"

The twenty-one teachers who write for this volume are excellent according to colleagues in the Departments of Education at their institutions. Their classroom success is acknowledged and appreciated. They are worthy of emulation. We can all learn from them. In the following pages they share what is behind what they do.

Reflections on Teaching

Lucy Cromwell (English)
Alverno College

I became a college teacher at the age of 22, barely out of a master's degree program. My first experience with a group of students came at an orientation session with new freshmen to discuss a book which they had been assigned to read during the summer. I can still remember the fear with which I entered the room. I sat down among the young students who were gathering and listened to them talk quietly; I had said nothing yet.

Finally, the time had come: I cleared my throat and announced that I was the teacher. The students were very surprised. At the time I thought they were surprised because I was so young; looking back, I suspect they were surprised because I was so quiet. I don't remember anything else about our discussion that day, except that I was focused entirely on how I felt and what I had to do there. If there is any one thing which marks me now as an excellent teacher it is that I place my emphasis on what my students are doing and not on myself. I concentrate on my students' involvement in their learning rather than on myself as the center of the classroom.

Ultimately, this deceptively simple shift in focus came to define my sense of quality teaching in higher education. I believe that excellent teaching is what we owe our students. They deserve nothing less than our full attention—on them, on their development, on their interaction with ideas and with each other. I leave it to others to determine the role of the research university in teaching undergraduate students; at

9

the liberal arts college, however, we must make teaching our primary responsibility.

In my own career, my strong sense of the importance of the student is the result of several key factors: teaching at Alverno College during the development of our ability-based curriculum, realizing the value of learning from my colleagues, and developing a personal philosophy about giving feedback to students. These three factors are closely connected, but bear separate examination as the description of my own development, and more importantly, as my prescription for excellence in college teaching.

When I came to Alverno College after a year of teaching in Colorado, I was only a bit more experienced as a teacher than I had been in that first group discussion. At first, I tried to emulate professors I had as an undergraduate. I remembered my awe in listening to a compelling lecture about Elizabethan drama, or my emotional involvement in hearing a professor carefully analyze a poem by Emily Dickinson. I tried to re-create that experience in my classrooms, spending many hours reading and synthesizing histories and works of criticism about my literary assignments. But while a few of my students had appropriately appreciative responses to my work, many others seemed only mildly interested. Some even had the audacity to question why we were spending time on Sophocles or Shaw.

My own assessment of the situation at the time was that I would never be the excellent teacher that I hoped to be; I would have to settle for a caring mediocrity. Luckily for me (and for my students), I became involved in a collaborative project which was to affect higher education across the country and certainly to change profoundly my life as an educator. In the early 1970's, the faculty of Alverno College began a reconceptualization of our curriculum.

Asking ourselves what it was that was most important for our students to learn, we developed a curriculum focused on eight abilities which students would develop across the entire curriculum. We worked together for several years to put in place a program that would allow students to graduate with a degree based not on a number of semester hours or courses, but on clearly developed ability in communication, analysis, problem solving, valuing in decision making, social interaction, effective citizenship, global responsibility, and aesthetic response, all studied in the context of liberal arts courses.

For me as a teacher, the underlying assumptions of our new curriculum were especially important in reshaping what it means for me to be an educator. Some of the key assumptions we articulated were that college education is as much a matter of developing certain life-long abilities as it is of attaining a certain body of knowledge, that the classroom—and indeed the entire curriculum—must be student-centered, and that students should learn, and be assessed according to, specified criteria that are made known to them.

As I attempted to incorporate specific work on communication, analysis, valuing, and aesthetic response into my classroom, I realized that I would have to balance my presentations of ideas and information with time for students to work on the abilities. Because I was still trying at that time to model myself after my best lecturing professors, I thought this might mean leaving time "at the end" to call for student participation or maybe building in some in-class writing exercises. Clearly I was still operating out of an assumption that I was the main actor in the classroom. Juggling my now conflicting goals, I became more and more convinced that the significant times in my class were those devoted to student involvement. I realized that it was time for the mediocre lecturer to disappear entirely. In place I have attempted to develop a teacher focused on each student's work toward specified abilities. I have become the manager of my classroom, the coach for each student, the developer of learning experiences designed to elicit specific abilities, the judge of student performance, the singer of students' praises, and the demander of achievement of high standards.

In short, I have become a teacher who looks at the classroom as an arena in which students learn, not as a place where I will be performing. In one sense, something has been lost: the thrilling performances that I remember from some of my best lecturers. On the other hand, though, I have opened up the classroom to the possibility of wonderful "performances" by students. Is there anything more thrilling to a teacher than a student demonstrating understanding of a concept, or applying an idea in a new context, or working with a group to interpret a difficult passage of a text? By placing emphasis on student achievement of ability, I have not really "given up" anything. Instead, I have gained a classroom atmosphere which is always alive with student thought and effort.

The concept that criteria for judgment of student performance should be made public is still strange to some, I am sure. Even more strange, unfortunately, is the idea that our teaching should be open to the scrutiny and evaluation of others. How has it happened that such a public activity, conducted before dozens of students, has become so secretive, so private? I feel fortunate that my experiences with the Alverno curriculum have put me in the position of working collaboratively with many colleagues—both in my own department and across disciplines. A primary reason for our emphasis on collaboration with peers is that in our effort to develop expertise in teaching for abilities we realized that strict discipline lines were not always the most effective way to organize our efforts. In developing techniques for teaching analytic ability, for example, I discovered that my colleagues in the sciences could teach me a great deal about helping students work with analytic models.

Likewise, I was able to help colleagues in other disciplines consider ways to use writing assignments and personal journals in non-traditional ways. The assistance we received from each other was so helpful, that we began to value feedback from peers about our teaching strategies and performance. Having a peer come into the classroom lost much of its ominous quality when we saw the positive benefits it could have. My own ability as a teacher, then, has been honed and improved by working with—and being evaluated by—my peers on the faculty.

The third factor in my development as an effective teacher is my growing understanding of the effect I have on my students through the feedback I give them on their work. Like many new English teachers, I was always quick with my editorial pen; no misplaced comma or misspelled word escaped my comment. As I studied theories of teaching writing, however, I learned the value of more descriptive feedback which focuses on a student's developing ability to convey a message, rather than detailed comments on each potential error. Additionally, I began to see how much more effective my positive feedback was. As we all know, students are far more likely to remember the negative comments they receive; one negative remark seems to have the power to erase all other observations. For the past few years I have been making a serious effort to give feedback which tells a student what has been done effectively, but which minimizes commentary on what is wrong or missing.

This is not as easy as it sounds. It is difficult to keep myself from immediately commenting on what the student has not done, what is not included which might have been appropriate, what would make the assignment better. If we remember that there will always be room for improvement in anyone's work (even our own) and that each assignment is part of an ongoing process, then it is a bit easier to forego the kind of criticism which highlights every mistake and omission made by a student.

Working with specific stated criteria has been of great help to me in developing my approach to positive feedback as well. I can say yes, the student has provided examples to support her/his ideas, and yes, the student has identified and clarified the sources of her/his thinking, and yes, the student has shown understanding of the relationships between literary elements, has applied a critical framework to a text. When I can do all that, I am less likely to structure my comments on the idea that the development of examples is not as thorough as it could be, or that the analytic reasoning is skimpy. I do include suggestions for future work, but I stress what has been accomplished rather than what has not. How many of us remember receiving a paper from an instructor and finding that the instructor has managed to discover our one typographical error . . . and nothing more. This detective approach to the reading of student papers or the study of their analytic work does little more than demoralize the student and frustrate the teacher. I believe it is my responsibility as a teacher to show a student what he/she has accomplished and how he/she is developing. Students have told me that they find my positive and non-threatening approach to feedback reassuring and supportive; I have found that students continue to improve in their performance. They have a sense of what they can build on rather than only what their deficiencies are.

When I consider the qualities which I believe define excellence in teaching, it seems that all of them involve a shift from traditional views to new ones: from a teacher-centered classroom to a student-centered one, from seeing teaching as a private and secretive enterprise to looking at it as a collaborative and public process, from telling students what they have done wrong to telling them what they are accomplishing as they work to achieve clearly-stated criteria. Perhaps these ideas are not really new, only overlooked in the complex atmosphere of the college campus.

Those of us who are committed to teaching undergraduates at liberal arts colleges must find ways to remember and reinstate an emphasis on student learning. We are there for them; they are not there for us. This sounds fairly obvious, and yet much of our graduate training continues to emphasize research and scholarship, not teaching. What other profession would stand for its major training to be in what might ultimately be a tangential or at least secondary area? I think back on myself as a newly educated college teacher. I knew about literary research and scholarship; I knew nothing about teaching. Because I had the good fortune to take a teaching position at a college which is dedicated to teaching and learning excellence, I have received the equivalent of another graduate degree in college teaching. But why must it be a lucky accident if we learn to teach well? We need to encourage the teaching activity as much as we encourage scholarship and research. Perhaps we need to make it our primary concern at the liberal arts college.

Certainly we will move toward such a goal by focusing our reward systems on teaching at the college level. Too many college teachers are still caught in the research and publishing web as they try to move forward in their careers. We must find ways to achieve some balance; perhaps we can start moving toward balance by tipping the scales toward teaching for a while.

14

Good Classroom Teaching is Good Conversation

John Oppelt (Mathematics and Computer Science)
Bellarmine College

Introduction

Good classroom teaching is good conversation. Good teaching in college is a lively discussion among all the faculty and students.

That would not describe my starting position when I entered graduate school in mathematics some years ago. Hindsight and reflection help me realize, however, that some seeds were planted then and nurtured over the years primarily by the conflict that exists between my love of mathematics and the uneven reception that I experience for the subject in and outside of the classroom.

This conflict is not peculiar to me or even to the field of mathematics. It can be ignored. As teachers we do this by adopting some form of elitism such as addressing the select few or reducing the course to a collection of basic facts. We also can ignore the conflict in our methodology such as an exclusive dependence on lecturing and the resulting derivatives in how we grade and evaluate.

Moreover, I discovered that my effectiveness as a teacher was dependent on broader concerns than those revolving around the learning of mathematics. The elements of learning, the drive to understand, the desire to make connections, the ability to analyze and problem solve, the inclination to explore and take chances, the empowerment derived from sound rhetoric, the opportunities that flow from failure, and the aspiration to be creative are all goals of the curriculum as a whole.

They are part of the broader discussion, not confined to one classroom or achievable by one professor in isolation. Their attainment is not apt to come about with the design of a curriculum and an occasional revision. The nature and background of the incoming student is too fluid as is the composition, education, and values of the faculty. Administrations change as do societal needs. Disciplines change in content, construction, applications, emphasis, and pedagogical approaches. So these curricular goals and the continuously changing nature of the players become sources of conflict not only because the fact that goals are set down for students and teachers but also because of the natural tendency for these goals to dim over time or seem to become irrelevant. We can also ignore these issues. We do this by devaluing course and curricular development, by discouraging team teaching, and by not systematizing interdisciplinary discussions and forums among our faculty or in our courses. Nor do we talk to, value, or promote interaction and alliances with teachers in the schools or between teacher educators and the other disciplines.

So I believe my effectiveness is a function of whether or not my teaching contains the elements of a good conversation, namely, content, a common vocabulary, sensitive listening, clarity of expression, asking questions without presuming answers, and a respect for those with whom I am conversing. It is also a function of how much attuned I am with my colleagues at the collegiate and school levels.

The Seeds

I doubt that my initial experience in teaching differs much from that of my peers. Upon my arrival at graduate school I found that I was assigned to teach a course designed to satisfy the core requirement of the non-science major. Here I was a college teacher when in reality, and certainly emotionally, I was an insecure student. Fortunately, one of the courses I took as a student turned out to be, and now I know was meant to be, one of those precious seeds. Arnold Ross, then chairperson of the department, taught the first year graduate students a course that might be described as explorations in mathematics. The methodology was give and take. He never allowed us to appeal to a known theorem. He was interested in developing a conversation with us to explore possible approaches and outcomes of problems posed by him. It was not a pedagogy that I was prepared to understand or put into practice. Except for some professorial help on test construction, I experienced no other instruction in methodology. On the other hand, there were several very good models. Professors who taught with enthusiasm, who placed the material in historical context, who left opened questions without being confusing, who drew parallels within the subject field, all proved important in my development. Moreover, I should not neglect those teachers who I experienced prior to graduate school and who stand out now, all of whom taught in a context broader than their particular course, who gave the impression that the subject in question was something to be treasured and who had a sense of who their students were.

On the Matter of Content (and Lecturing)

The same Arnold Ross delivered one of those trivial, but nonetheless memorable statements, "Bad teachers teach more than they know; good teachers teach much less than they know." When I teach a course in a subject that lies close to the edge of my knowledge, the classroom conversation disappears. My lectures are meticulously prepared (which in and of itself says something about the lecture method). Connections to other subject fields and within mathematics are rare. I become more the authority even though I am dealing with a subject on which I am less the authority. The student becomes the receiver (if the switch remains in the 'on' position).

This same phenomenon, authority/receiver, lecturer/listener, becomes the reality when I resort to the lecture for prolonged periods of time. Now as a classroom lecturer I do accomplish a form of listening much like a performer plays the audience. The classical student reactions are telltale signs of their involvement in or distance from what is being unfolded. It remains, however, an inherently passive form of learning.

17

As a lecturer I can certainly demonstrate multiple paths for approaching the subject, including false starts, and then demonstrate those higher order thinking skills that lead to a solution. Still, it is more "Let's see how I would . . ." rather than "Why don't we try . . ." I surely remove any possibility of acting as a knowledgeable consultant to individuals or small groups who are exploring possibilities on their own. As a lecturer only, it is easy to pose questions but impossible to act as a moderator and protagonist of a class discussion.

Moreover, preservice teachers in a class where I serve as the authoritative dispenser of knowledge will be inclined to teach as they have been taught. They are not apt to pose questions to their class for consideration and decision making. They will not see the value in cooperative learning and student exploration. Indeed, even though these methodologies may be taught to them in their professional courses, the methods will tend to remain theoretical if they are not confirmed in their content courses. Here we have a prime example of the broader dimensions of good college teaching that I mentioned. If the teacher education that preservice students receive in their professional courses is in conflict with the teaching they experience in content courses, how can we expect the students to mesh the two? They are bound to remain separate concepts. Indeed, I believe they put students in the position of choosing between the two, even if it be a subconscious choice. This situation gives meaning to the argument of "what is more important, method or content." It is as foolish and misguided an argument as the one that revolves around "publish or perish."

It does not necessarily follow that research, or more precisely, publishing research makes for good teaching. The work can be too far removed from the classroom, can distract from teaching obligations or the professor may simply never integrate the research into the syllabus. Nor does it necessarily follow that research makes for bad teaching. It is intellectually stimulating, nurtures the creative juices, looks to the future, and makes for a fuller understanding of the subject matter. It does follow that an emphasis on published research in tenure, promotion and merit decisions—to the exclusion of other scholarly activities may not produce the classroom teacher that an undergraduate liberal arts college needs.

The most powerful and consistent positive message that comes from the student evaluations of my classes has been described as an infectious enthusiasm about mathematics. I know my excitement about the subject derives from my continuing study of mathematics in terms of its content, in terms of its historical development and the creative individuals who were the participants. This enthusiasm also derives not only from its applications, as a language and as a means to model phenomena, but also how applications have caused it to develop, and have supplied the creative force. Finally it stems from an active involvement with those who teach and use and "do" the subject. For me that continuing study has taken the form of research and publication, involvement in the professional societies and their meetings, reading the journals (including those that concentrate on essays and teaching approaches), and active participation in colloquia. It also includes being an equal partner in alliances with teachers at elementary, middle and secondary levels.

On Listening

If my beginnings as a teacher of mathematics could be described as an effort to learn the subject well enough to talk about it, then the middle of my development might be described as an effort to understand what and how the listener hears. At one time I believed that a student's success was completely dependent on what I said, how well it was delivered, and how much effort he or she was willing to exert. I also believed that a student's failure, assuming I delivered well, was totally a function of the student's own lack of effort and attention. (I never have believed that the learning of mathematics is the preserve of the talented few.)

Later I began to pay attention to the limitations students imposed upon themselves, and what expectations they had of me or of mathematics itself. Their experiences with learning in general and mathematics in particular became important variables for me to know.

It is impossible to consider the teaching and learning of my discipline and not come to grips with the experiences of women in the mathematics classroom. The assumptions made by all

19

segments of our society—the interests suppressed as inappropriate—are nothing short of criminal. Math anxiety may not be owned by women alone, but they certainly bear the greatest burden. And this burden is most evident in the content courses of elementary school programs. (In a recent discussion I had with an English professor, she referred to my poetry anxiety. For perverse reasons, it was good to hear that it existed though not that I had contracted it.)

Since students were turning their listening switches off no matter how well I performed or attempted to engage them within the context of my lecture, that conflict between my love of the subject and its reception demanded that I engage them in a different way, certainly in a way that allowed for more individual variations. A sequence of acknowledged successes is the surest way to break down artificial but real barriers and to dissipate math anxiety. In order to accomplish this I needed to know how I could set them up for a success, one that they would know to be real. Similarly, I needed to have a basis to offer them alternative explanations with which they were comfortable. Nor could I accept the students' own self-imposed limitations. They had to be challenged to respond, to want to respond and not hide. Standard testing does not constitute this challenge to respond. Moreover, students hide on tests and in doing so fulfill their own expectations.

Who Else Is Talking

If I consistently ask myself what it is that excites me about mathematics, what are the creative highlights, what are the connections to other parts of mathematics or to other fields to which this branch can be applied as a model, what are the historical problems that were solved, and why did this piece of mathematics evolve, then this reflection has the effect of maintaining my classroom enthusiasm. As a result I deliver a wonderful lecture. Further reflection points out that my enthusiasm is a result of my own discoveries and because I made the connections and saw the modeling opportunities. There is no doubt that my own teachers have provided a less fettered road to where I am today; that their excitement was contagious. Nonetheless, it is my own explorations, discoveries, aborted attempts and successes, halting explanations to others, which are the significant stepping stones to where I stand today in my discipline. To me, this is what constitutes the other part of the conversation. I have come to believe that it is wrong to leave this part to chance in my classroom. It is too exclusive. Students almost have to have the "disease" before you infect them. Pity the poor students who come to you anxious about the subject, bored with it, predisposed that it is irrelevant or is seriously distracted. They need to be engaged in a personal way. They need to be allowed to find solutions, but attempts lead to good thinking. They need to be able to explore possible extensions and experience the satisfaction of discovery. All students need the opportunity to display their particular strengths, for example, in cooperative learning as a member of a team. They need the discipline of writing correctly about what they have accomplished, documenting their work so that others can follow up. They need to be prodded to explain their work verbally if for no other reason than to clarify their own thinking.

It becomes my job to encourage these activities, to create the moment and choose the setting so that these activities have a positive impact upon them. To do this I need to engage them in a way that is different than just being a presumed interested party in the front of the room. I need to know them individually as best I can at least on the level of what they think they know, what they think they can learn, and what they think is important. In short I need to know what limitations they have imposed upon themselves so that I have the opportunity to expand the fences, if not trample them down altogether.

There is a derivative favor I do my students if I can promote these activities in my courses. I know of no work situation, including the life of teaching and research, that does not operate without teamwork. Business today begs colleges to produce people who can explore, verbalize, write, cooperate, and provide a positive and confident input in their work settings. Then there is the favor I do my colleagues in philosophy, teacher education, language, science, rhetoric, logic, economics, and social sciences. My classroom no longer exists for me alone or for mathematics alone. If done right, students should not walk into or out of my classroom unconnected.

The Liberal Arts College

The opportunity for me to conduct my teaching in such a "connected" fashion may not be completely dependent upon the fact that I profess in a liberal arts college setting, though my experience tells me it is much more possible. I believe, however, that I have the obligation to do so because I am in this setting.

I recently attended a conference on value education. A university dean expounded on the exclusiveness of his own classroom. Whatever came before, even the immediate hour before, was meaningless. Importance and value was solely a function of his class. That is certainly not the ballpark where I want to play. The concept of a campus being a collection of scholars to whom the students go and receive their particular brand of wisdom surely has its following and might have its place. But in and of itself, it presupposes mature learners who create their own syllabi and formulate their own senior seminars.

I believe that good classroom teaching is the obligation of the liberal arts college and should be the merit basis of all of its faculty's activities. I believe that good classroom teaching is a function of shared values and a shared vision of its faculty. I believe that these shared values and vision are a product of the faculty's current knowledge of and participation in a coherent curriculum. To this end it is the obligation of the liberal arts college to focus its merit system on classroom teaching and to relate both internal and external service as well as scholarly activity primarily in this regard. It is incumbent upon the liberal arts college to provide an evaluation system of its faculty and curriculum that is complete (taking into consideration the viewpoints of present students, past students, peers, the subject field, as well as the goals of the curriculum and of the college) and that is helpful (so that it is accompanied by a developmental program for both its new and experienced faculty). The college should provide the time and opportunity for its faculty to convene in appropriate forums to provide the opportunity for them to formulate values and visions, to understand and learn the pedagogy present and possible in the different disciplines and to come to grips with the shared responsibilities in the curriculum. In particular this ought to include the development of methodologies to promote good written and verbal communication, sound analysis and problem solving techniques, and appropriate and actual use of technology.

Administrations need to develop their own philosophy if these priorities are to be accepted in fact (e.g.,monetarily) and not simply in word. To do this they need to be part of the discussion, indeed take a leadership role in making the discussion possible. It does not promote the common welfare of good teaching if the external affairs office extols only the most recent publication and the business office questions the expenses of developmental seminars and reduced loads. The president needs to prod the faculty to become the college's major resource and take a leadership role to provide the means and encourage the faculty to attain that goal. The dean needs to allow and encourage experiments with alternate approaches and strategies in the classroom as well as discussions of the issues in the teaching and learning across disciplines, and promote opportunities for the faculty to maintain and grow in their knowledge base.

On Teacher Education

The liberal arts college is dealt a winning hand in the education and training of teachers. Their teacher educators and content professors do not have to endure the chasm built on years of misunderstanding and cemented by the structure of separate and distant academic units. Because of the intimacy and efficiencies within which the faculty of liberal arts colleges work, the education and training of preservice teachers can and should become the shared responsibility of the entire faculty.

My experience suggests that the leadership role belongs to the teacher educators. Their knowledge base, their involvement in the schools and community contacts, their mandates from accrediting organizations, and their bottom line commitment to produce school educators of lasting quality demands this. My own involvement with the National Council of Teachers of Mathematics (NCTM) and its local affiliates was initiated through my workshop collaboration with one of Bellarmine's teacher educators and her school contacts. Entrance into school classrooms has been made possible by the evaluation component of our teacher education programs. My service on the Teacher Education Committee is by invitation of that department. The evolution of my teaching in the preparation course of our elementary school program is due to countless discussions with our teacher educators and with those in other colleges where I served. And it is most important to add that my evolution as a teacher in all of my mathematics courses is a direct outcome of the experiments and changing strategies I undertook in the elementary teacher course.

I am now aware of and am an active participant in the significant and exciting approaches suggested by the recent publications of The Mathematical Association of America, The Mathematics Science Education Board, NCTM, and the National Research Council. I am more keenly sensitive to the Kentucky Education Reform Act and have had a greater chance to contribute to its unfolding in the schools than the ordinary citizen or mathematics professor. I am therefore more aware of the broader implications of the collegiate changes in calculus and the mathematics major now being promoted by my professional societies. I trace this awareness to my continuing involvement with our teacher educators and to the alliances I form with school teachers of science and mathematics.

So, with leadership provided by professional educators, methodology and content courses can be better coordinated, involvement and alliances with the schools and the collegiate faculty can be facilitated, issue forums can be systematically scheduled, and memberships in teaching societies can be promoted.

Summary

Just as I believe my classroom is better if it contains the elements of good conversation, so too I believe a student's collegiate experience is more coherent, more challenging and of greater value if the elements of good conversation are a basis of the faculty's unified effort. So too, the administration must be part of and should encourage that systematic interchange. These approaches are particularly important between educationists and teachers of the content areas for the promotion of effective teaching on the part of our graduates.

Conversation and Controversy: Teaching the Humanities Today

Marcia A. McDonald (English)
Belmont University

Hℴw much John Donne do I lop off to get in Lady Mary Wortley Montagu? Do I ask my students to buy a paperback so I can introduce them to an underread Shakespearean comedy instead of the anthology's oft-assigned tragedy? Such is the late night wrestling this English teacher does with her ideal reading list for British Lit and the practical realities of the semester system and literature anthologies.

I do my wrestling with two concerns in mind: How will I make these works engaging to a group of sophomores meeting general education requirements? What statement am I making about the place of this literature in culture? The first question may seem a respectable, pragmatic concern; the second, a grandiose preoccupation best left to scholarly essays. But the task of teaching English—indeed all of the humanities—in the 1990s has made both of these questions relevant, and relevant to each other. In order to teach with integrity, I have to answer both questions as best I can, and my syllabus is the first effort at an answer.

The relationship between my particular classes and the larger context of teaching in the humanities was not a concern when I started teaching—but at that time reading lists of literature courses were not the concern of the *Wall Street Journal, The New York Times,* government officials, and book publishers. In recent years, a series of best sellers with surprisingly long and esoteric titles (*The Closing of the American Mind: How Higher Education Has Failed Democracy and Impoverished the Souls of Today's Students; Cultural Literacy: What Every American Needs to Know*) have led to heated debates on and off campus, making the humanities classroom front page news. "Multiculturalism vs. the western tradition," "literary theory vs. literature," "feminism vs. the canon," all these topics are now the lingo of the news media as much as of academic circles.

While a "versus" mentality can be debilitating in a teaching community, it can also spur the individual teacher to reassess his or her classroom and pedagogy, as it has done for me. I have renewed my commitment to the classroom as conversation and have gained new perspectives on the place of the humanities in culture. Most importantly, I have an awareness of what I am doing and why. It is this awareness that I want to communicate to my students. This awareness also makes it possible to articulate the value of teaching to colleagues as well as to prospective teachers.

I: The Classroom as Conversation

When I try to describe my teaching, I instinctively look for metaphors or stories—not unusual for an English teacher, for those are my stock in trade. My primary metaphor for teaching is "conversation." I hear myself saying "we got into a good discussion about this poem"; "the students had a heated exchange about that novel"; "we went round and round about that topic"; and "class was a real dud today—the silence was deafening." I do believe that the language in comments like these, comments in the banter with colleagues around the coffee pot in the faculty lounge, reveal more about assumptions and practice in the classroom than more formally phrased descriptions on syllabi or self-evaluation forms. "Conversation" may seem a trivial description of a carefully-crafted Socratic method of teaching that I work very hard to implement. In Kenneth Burke's terms, however, conversation is what all of us are engaged in who try to make sense of our world:

26

> Imagine that you enter a parlor. You come late. When you arrive, others have long preceded you, and they are engaged in a discussion too heated for them to pause and tell you exactly what it is about. In fact, the discussion had already begun long before any of them got there, so that no one present is qualified to retrace for you all the steps that had gone before. You listen for a while, until you decide that you have caught the tenor of the argument; then you put in your oar. Someone answers; you answer back . . .[1]

As a college teacher, my goal is to enable my students to join that conversation and to recognize some patterns that conversation takes. To realize that goal, I must give students significant responsibility in creating the particular classroom colloquy that is our local conversation, and I must give them a context, a perspective from which to measure our classroom conversation.

Enacting the conversation metaphor in the classroom requires students to assume responsibility for generating the matter of the class. Reading and writing assignments lay the groundwork for the process of the classroom: the exchange and debate of ideas and interpretations. I gear my reading and writing assignments to the classroom: the students will bring ideas based on readings, and take away ideas to explore in their writing, which then feeds back in to the classroom in later readings and writings.

The classroom as conversation, the Socratic method which establishes the teacher as question-poser rather than answer-giver, does have its detractors, and rightly so. Where is the real authority in the classroom? Isn't the teacher's authority, so obvious in that final grade roster, merely hidden behind the guise of a round-table discussion? Yes, it can be unless the teacher discloses the classroom processes as carefully as the reading list or the details of a line in a poem. The way of teaching as well as the "whats" of the subject are matter for the classroom. First day statements of rationale should resurface in relationship to particular assignments or discussions. The goal of such revelation is not to reveal the teacher's private personality, but rather to increase awareness on everyone's part of the process of developing and transmitting knowledge.

The second charge leveled against the classroom as conversation is that it depends upon responsible students, and rarely are all students in a class equally dependable. True, but the fact that some students lack responsibility at a certain stage of their lives does not make them any less responsible for their education. The goal of my teaching is to promote a long-term engagement with the humanities and with learning, beyond the confines of a classroom, a syllabus, a semester. That can more likely result from a classroom format that requires students to be active rather than passive. I would rather take risks with a format that some students may resist in order to reach my long-term goal than settle for secure patterns that may make students too comfortable with their college educations.

Creating a classroom as a conversation, especially as Burke describes above, means there will be unanswered questions, unexplained positions. But the conversation is not a free-for-all, where all opinions are equally valid. There is the need to listen attentively to the conversation, to catch its tenor and parameters, before one can join with confidence. Especially for the teacher, this means attention to current scholarship about the subject. In the classroom as conversation, it is imperative that the teacher be engaged as much as possible with the current conversations in one's area. New facts and new interpretations are the shield against the solipsistic repetition of one's favorite opinions. I hope my classroom opens up, not closes off a subject, and my students master not a product as much as a process. I believe that these result from having our opinions challenged by the arguments of others. Such is the value of teaching the humanities in a time of controversy, when the debates force one's assumptions into the clear to be scrutinized by teacher, students, and colleagues alike.

II: Teaching the Controversy

Each generation feels the professional and philosophical issues of its moment, the debates that pull the rug out from under our assumptions, that leave us bare, that make us reassess the "whys" of our profession, our discipline, our institution. Such periods are not time for retreat, but for engagement, for they offer great opportunities to increase our self-

awareness and to formulate effective rationales for our practices—not to mention gain new ideas and insights and change
our minds! This is how I see current state of affairs in the
teaching of the humanities. Yes, it is odd to read about one's
"ivory tower" profession regularly on the pages of national
newspapers; on the other hand, such publicity makes the issue
of the relevance of literature and the humanities a moot point
for students nowadays. These debates provide the lens for the
long look that each local classroom needs—the look into why
we're reading these selections; what people have thought "literature" was; what this idea, or character, or language meant
in its day and means in ours; why a conversation is a way of
acquiring knowledge about the humanities.

The current debates, some complain, have politicized teaching by encouraging the view that all choices on a syllabus are
political choices. But this is not a valid complaint. The debates
have pointed out how the disciplines in the humanities evolve.
The humanities, including literature, are not repositories of
facts but of struggles over interpretations and categories. Play
texts were not "literature" in early modern England, so Shakespeare did not make it into Oxford's Bodleian Library. How did
Shakespeare get into the category of great literature? Likewise, is the "Gettysburg Address" literature? Wonderful prose,
but it was intended as a eulogy. So why is it in every standard
anthology of American Literature? And John Donne virtually
disappeared from view in the eighteenth and nineteenth cen-
turies. We have many such examples of our changing tastes,
standards, categories. I may accept or resist the notion that
my syllabus is a political document, but I ignore the charge at
the risk of fossilizing myself and my students. Their children
will see a different syllabus in their college literature courses.
I hope they can enjoy a good exchange of ideas about what
people think literature is these days, rather than butting
heads about whether new Professor Trend's syllabus is better
than old Professor McDonald's!

While the debates alert us to the biases in our individual
syllabi and provide the vehicle for contextualizing a class
discussion, they should not be brought into the class as po-
lemic. Such a strategy would, of course, stifle the conversation.
Instead, as students pursue the larger questions that the

current debates frame for them, they gain a handle on the big picture that is their education, and they should be free to draw their own conclusions. Students need road maps and compasses—that's what teachers can provide—but their final destination is their own. By realizing that their local classroom is a small part of a vast intellectual and political landscape, the aware students can light out on their own.

III: Educating Teachers

It is entirely possible that in a few years this essay will sound dated. Surely the current intense debate will cool somewhat, and journalists and publishing houses will lose interest in the state of the humanities and the fate of the liberal arts curriculum. But that does not mean that we as teachers will no longer be compelled to justify our choices or to recognize the relationship of our classroom to the world external to it. Each generation will have its controversy. However, a teacher's need for self-awareness is perennial. Such awareness comes with professional maturation, but I believe we can encourage it in prospective primary, secondary, and college teachers. Their awareness of the relationship between their particular practices and the central issues of their discipline and of education can give them the confidence to make responsible choices in their classrooms and within their profession.

The theories and programs of "reflective teaching" developed over the past decade are one means to enable the novice teacher to gain insights into his or her practices and classroom.[2] For those of us working with prospective teachers in our own disciplines, the debates over our discipline are another effective means to this awareness. We should invite prospective teachers into the current debates as full partners in the conversation. We should let the debates shake their assumptions. And we should offer them a steadying hand in our own candor, honesty, and fairness.

Lest the "steadying hand" factor sounds sentimental, let me suggest that it is the key link in a series of bridges we must build between our colleges and universities and our primary and secondary schools. On the one hand, it may seem deceitful to send out thoughtful and self-aware teachers, ready to critique their own pedagogy, into overcrowded classrooms in underfunded schools. But on the other hand, the teacher who begins a career with some perspective on a discipline and on the educational process as a whole—who has along with notebooks full of facts the lived experience of shaping a body of knowledge—that teacher may be less likely to accept things as they are, and more likely to marshall resources to change what can be changed and do the best with what cannot. Someday her students may engage in life already responsible for their own learning.

The dialogue between my local classroom and the national controversies makes teaching compelling for me. In conversations with students, I am always confronting something new. Even similar ideas will be phrased in different language. My responses in the conversation are drawn in part from the way I think our particular moment reflects the larger context, the national debates. My responses also reveal why I think as I do about a topic. And just as I ask students to work through their own assumptions that lead them to their conclusions, I have to judge anew the validity of my perspective. While this thinking and re-thinking goes on day after day, class after class, the moments of intense conversation are few. Some semesters are completely dry; other classes are bountiful. But the conversations are worth pursuing for the sake of the one or two with a group of students that will be landmarks. The discussion of Douglass' *Narrative of the Life of an American Slave* with an American Literature class in 1990; of the Wife of Bath with a Chaucer class in 1987; John Stuart Mill's essays with a British Literature class in 1986; *Waiting for Godot* with a freshman class in 1978; everything with a freshman class in 1984!— these are among the conversations I remember, and of which students remind me. Such a handful of successes may not be much to measure a teaching strategy by, but that any exist at all is for me a validation of the conversation metaphor. For the conversations listed above are ones that continue with students from these classes as I see or hear from them. Such lifelong engagement was my initial goal.

I will lop off some of the John Donne so Lady Mary Wortley Montagu's voice can get in the conversation. And I will order the paperback *Midsummer Night's Dream* so that Bottom can mangle everyone's notion of propriety in love-making and play-making. And I look forward to the conversation someday with an alumna who says, "You know those John Donne poems you took off the British Lit syllabus back in 1991? Well, I've been reading them . . ."

Notes

1. Burke, K. (1967). *The philosophy of literary form*, 2nd ed. Baton Rouge: Louisiana State University Press, 110.
2. See the work by D. A. Schon (1990). *Educating the reflective practitioner*. San Francisco: Jossey-Bass; D. A. Schon (1983). *The reflective practitioner*. New York: Basic Books. See also J. Gore (1987). Reflecting on reflective teaching, *Journal of Teacher Education, 38*, 33–39, and the entire fortieth volume (1989) of the *Journal of Teacher Education*.

Teaching Science and the Liberal Arts

Daniel Schroeder (Physics and Astronomy)
Beloit College

As I began thinking about the dual themes to be addressed in this paper, the role of quality teaching in a liberal arts college and what it is that I believe makes an effective teacher, I at first wondered what profound wisdom I could share with the reader. I soon decided that any attempt to be profound was doomed to failure because in my experience there is no set of magic formulas which, if followed, guarantee excellent teaching. Different persons use different approaches and what works for one teacher may not be the best method for another. There is no single recipe which can be codified as the way to teach for all subject areas and all levels of students.

Having come to this conclusion, I decided to simply describe what it is that I try to do to promote learning in and out of the classroom. I will discuss some of the precepts which guide my approach to teaching in the classroom and laboratory, and particular techniques which have been successful for me in helping students learn. After all, this is all that finally matters—to help students to learn—and whatever success I have had is based on keeping this goal firmly in mind when working with them.

The approach to teaching any subject area is determined, at least in part, by the nature of that subject. In my case the subjects are physics and astronomy, and it is necessary to say a bit about the characteristics of these disciplines and how these help shape my teaching. Physics is a discipline in which the aim is to understand the fundamental units of which matter is composed—atoms, electrons, the zoo of fundamental particles—and to use this knowledge to explain quantitatively phenomena seen in the natural world. It is a codified body of knowledge with well-defined laws and principles which have been developed over hundreds of years, and embodied in the major subfields of mechanics, electromagnetism, thermodynamics, relativity, and quantum theory. Each of these theories is based on relatively few sets of laws or principles expressed in mathematical form which, in turn, are used to explore the workings of the world around us. The aim then is to use these theories to account quantitatively for the vast variety of experimental and observational information which has been gathered.

Astronomy is that part of physics which deals with the universe and its component parts—planets, stars, galaxies, clusters of galaxies—and uses all of the theories of physics in an attempt to understand their workings. In one important respect astronomy is unique in that it is an observational science as opposed to an experimental one. The objects whose workings astronomers seek to understand cannot be synthesized in the lab and tinkered with; they can only be observed as they are found in nature.

Given the vast range of phenomena which physicists and astronomers seek to understand, how then can one teach students what it is that is important and essential? How can one get them to see the forest and not get lost in the trees? One important aspect which I emphasize is that physics and astronomy are not static bodies of knowledge but are dynamic and subject to change and extension. The theories are subject to revision as new information is gathered and the continual interplay between theory and observation or experimentation is the heart of these disciplines. A second important theme is the application of what is known to the unknown. This, in turn, requires that problem solving on the part of students and not simply memorization of isolated facts is paramount. Understanding is only achieved when students apply the known basic principles to new situations.

These points are best illustrated by an example. The orbit of a planet around the sun and the falling of an apple to the ground are governed by the same principle, the force of gravity present between bodies which possess mass. This principle was first enunciated in quantitative form by Newton over three hundred years ago. Since that time this principle has been used to explain the nature of binary stars, pairs of stars in mutual revolution around one another; the motions of stars such as the sun within our galaxy; the motions of galaxies within clusters of galaxies; and the grand design of the universe itself. In each of these cases the application of a known principle to a new phenomenon has led to increased understanding. This work, in turn, has also led to modifications of the law of gravity as put forth by Newton and expressed by Einstein in the theory of general relativity.

My approach in the classroom to all of this is a mix of discussion of basic concepts and illustrative examples (problem solving). I try to show how one uses what is known to get answers to questions—using the known to explore the unknown. The aim is showing by example the approach which is necessary to understand how science advances.

The discussion of basic concepts requires dealing with precisely defined abstractions such as energy, momentum, velocity, and acceleration. It is often difficult for students to grasp the meaning of these abstractions and to apply them, hence demonstrations and models are a key element in helping them. Simple examples are the use of a ball rolling down an inclined plane to illustrate acceleration, as first used by Galileo to understand this concept, and the use of a celestial sphere to demonstrate the rising and setting of the sun and stars relative to one's horizon. The use of models and demonstrations makes the abstract more concrete.

Another aspect of my subject areas is the disparity between the sizes of the objects being studied and the objects with which students are familiar. In physics we often deal with the very small, such as atoms or fundamental particles; in astronomy we deal with the very large, such as the solar system or vast complexes of stars. In these cases the use of scale models helps to make the abstract more concrete.

As an example consider our solar system, the sun plus planets and moons. Distances such as Earth to moon of 240,000 miles or Earth to sun of 93,000,000 miles are far larger than any distance we have any feeling for, and a scale model can help make these distance more real. For example, define a scale factor which reduces the distance from the Earth to the sun to 20 feet. Now the sun is about the size of an orange and the Earth is the size of the tip of a ballpoint pen. The moon is a speck of dust about one-half inch from the Earth and is the distance humankind has traveled into the vast universe! In this same model the most distant planet, Pluto, is 800 feet from the sun and the nearest star is about 1000 miles from Earth. Another way to illustrate the immensity of these distances is to assume a spaceship traveling at 100,000 miles per hour. At this rate it takes a little over two hours to reach the moon, nearly five years to reach Pluto, and about 30,000 years to get to the nearest star! The initially incomprehensible distances with which astronomers deal are thus brought into a range which students can begin to comprehend.

As a second example consider a typical atom and imagine it is expanded to fill a large football stadium such as the Rose Bowl. The electrons which swarm around the nucleus are no larger than specks of dust in this model and the nucleus itself is about the size of a small BB in the center of the stadium. Most of the atom is empty space! Again, this is another way to help students get a grasp of something which is outside their direct range of experiences.

The application of known principles to new situations in solving problems and the generation of scale models by the students themselves have proven to be effective teaching tools, and I use them extensively for homework assignments. I also try to construct exams in a similar way. For example, an exam covering solar systems will not deal specifically with our planets and moons but will instead be built around a hypothetical solar system involving planet X and moon M. The students are expected to apply what they have learned to a new situation. In this way I try to reinforce what it is that scientists do: the application of the known in an attempt to understand something new.

In the lab or observatory my approach is one of promoting self-discovery by students. For example, rather than having students look through a single telescope at an object and explaining to them what it is they are seeing, I have pairs of students observe with separate telescopes. They are given a list of objects to look for and are asked to observe for themselves. In this way they discover that stars have different colors or spectra which, in turn, they can connect with something they learned in the classroom: that stars have different temperatures. Observations such as these reinforce concepts discussed in the classroom and give a reality to what often are only abstractions.

Although the above examples are specific to my subject areas, I suspect the approaches can prove useful in any number of disciplines.

There are also a few somewhat more general precepts which I have found important in my teaching. First, I try to use a distinctive approach and to follow it with enthusiasm. I try always to put a different slant on the topic under discussion, if only to demonstrate to the students that the approach in a textbook is not necessarily the only one. Second, I try to keep in mind that I once was in that seat. What questions did I have when I first encountered this subject? What concepts did I find particularly difficult? Having taught several dozen classes of introductory students, it is sometimes hard to recall those days as a student, but the attempt must be made. Third, I remind myself that "They're Not Dumb, They're Different." This is the title of a book by Sheila Tobias which emphasizes that different students have different modes of learning. What is easy for one student may be difficult for another, and vice versa, and I try to accommodate these differences. Finally, I try to emphasize encouragement and constructive criticism to help students learn. It is easy simply to mark an answer wrong and leave it at that; it takes more time to show where a wrong track has been taken and why, but in the end the latter approach is much better for promoting learning.

Much of the above is a personal statement on my own teaching style and what I have found effective over the years. With this as background, I want to discuss more generally the role of first-rate teaching in liberal arts colleges. Books have been written on this subject, but I will be brief.

Education and the development of independent thinkers is our reason for being, and excellent teaching is the best way I know of for reaching this goal. Each of us has had one or more

37

role models whose excellent teaching was a significant contributor to our intellectual development and whose influence
continued long after a particular class was over. By inspiration
and example we were stimulated to continue learning beyond
the formal work done in a given course. In my view there is
nothing more important than developing the habits of lifelong
learning, and first-rate teaching is a key element in doing this.
This is especially true in the education of future teachers who
will have a major impact on their students at whatever level.
The seeds planted by an excellent teacher at a liberal arts
college can be multiplied many times as future teachers go on
to influence students of their own.

Untitled

David Oswald (Communications and Theatre Arts)
Cardinal Stritch College

Three years ago at Cardinal Stritch College, I was invited to join a task force on effective teaching. The goals of the group were to reaffirm and support the college's emphasis on quality classroom teaching and to create and implement an effective evaluation process that would be consistent across the campus. As part of the group's final report, a definition of the effective teacher was drafted. It reads, as follows: "The effective teacher is one who enables and assists students to progress toward and attain their educational goals." This definition is followed by a list of ten personal and professional qualities demonstrated by the effective teacher. They include "a caring, sensitive, open-minded attitude toward the individual student; commitment to the liberal arts by integrating subject matter with other disciplines, the outside world and future career opportunities; genuine interest in and enthusiasm for the course content; confidence and poise; creativity and reasonable flexibility; preparation and organization; fair and reasonable treatment of students; continued professional growth incorporating self-evaluation; support of professional peers; and accountability for professional responsibilities."

As definitions go, this is an excellent and comprehensive one, providing an ideal to which all of us can aspire; but teaching is a profession of doing, and any definition, no matter how excellent, cannot address how each of us individually meet the daily challenges of interacting with students and motivating them to grow and learn in the college classroom environment.

I remember vividly my first day of college teaching over thirteen years ago. Filled with nervous anxiety over whether my students would like and approve of me, the climb up the stairs to the second floor classroom seemed to take an eternity. I'm not sure that first day went that well, but as I return to the classroom each semester I am still filled with that same sense of nervous energy, but now I am exhilarated by the possibilities that await me as well as the students.

I have had many successes in the classroom over the past thirteen years and I attribute these successes to several reasons. The first, and perhaps most important, is the fact that I passionately love my content area of theatre. Whether I am teaching the conventions of ancient Greek theatre and their applications to Sophocles' *Oedipus Rex*, coaching two actors through a difficult scene from *Twelfth Night*, or discussing a production concept with a student designer, I have great commitment and passion for the task at hand.

Good teaching involves role-modeling in two very specific ways: demonstrating a love of content and its practice, and showing an insatiable desire for continued learning and growth. In my discipline, where teachers work so closely with their students, colleagues will argue that it is easy to impassion the learner; but I would argue that I have observed many outstanding colleagues in diverse disciplines motivate and inspire their students through their example of passion for the content. A good and competent teacher is enthusiastic; the outstanding instructor is passionate.

More than passion, however, is required in successful teaching. My growth and maturity as a teacher owes much to the influence of colleagues who have nurtured me in very positive ways. I teach at an institution where quality teaching is valued as the first priority. Thus, colleagues talk teaching on a regular, if not daily, basis. Coaching and mentoring of junior faculty is an integral part of our work as educators. Several years ago I joined a four-person coaching team made up of two colleagues from the Education Division and one from our department. We all knew each other very well and had a sense of mutual professional respect, but we had never observed each other in the classroom. It was a paradoxical situation, frightening and yet challenging. All four of us had reputations on campus as excellent teachers, so this was not an attempt to show off for one another, but a sincere attempt to get valuable feedback on our individual methodologies in the classroom.

We worked together for an entire academic year and our collaboration proved to be one of the most positive experiences of my teaching career. The primary focus in each of the classroom visits was to identify the positives for each teacher. Prior to each visit the instructor being observed presented the members of the team with instructional objectives and the strategies to be employed. The instructor asked each of the visiting teachers to observe a specific aspect of teaching such as nonverbal presentation, paralinguistic effectiveness, group activity strategies, and the appropriateness of discussion questions in terms of student responses.

This experience was helpful to me for a variety of reasons. First, it reinforced the positives of my classroom instruction and helped me to understand why certain techniques were working better than others. Secondly, it provided me with some concrete strategies to improve my teaching which renewed my excitement for my profession. Finally, it taught me a new respect for my colleagues, who while sharing their expertise, revealed their authenticity to me. I continue to serve as a mentor and coach, not only because it provides me with the opportunity to enable my colleagues (teachers teaching teachers if you will), but because it has provided me with the opportunity for professional development and growth.

The more time I spend in the classroom, the less content - driven I have become. Students today, because of our MTV, image-oriented culture, have become more passive learners. If they are to become engaged and assume ownership for their learning, I have found that less lecture and more group activities produce more significant results. In teaching the discipline of acting, we say, "acting is doing." It is a vital and active process in which the student must participate. This is true not just in the arts, but in any discipline we teach. The student *will* become more engaged in the learning situation if we, as teachers, ask them to assume responsibility, not only for what they learn, but what their classmates are learning.

One of the most successful techniques I have utilized, which was suggested to me by one of my colleagues, is assigning a small group of students the responsibility for a particular topic. They are required to master and present with coherency these materials to the remainder of the class. As instructor, I am no longer required to lecture on this material, but rather my role becomes one of facilitator, suggesting organizational as well as presentational techniques (handouts, visual aids, etc.) to the students. In addition, I help guide the discussion and question-and-answer period that follows, asking the students to clarify topics and raise salient points that they have missed in their presentation. The student is no longer a passive notetaker, but a teacher. The result is that the student now has empathy for the instructor, and the classroom has become an environment of reciprocity between student and student. The classroom now belongs to the students and I have become an "enabler."

For me, spontaneity and creativity remain the key to keeping my classroom an exciting place. In my dramatic literature class, I make the following statement in my syllabus: "This is a discussion, not a lecture course. Consequently the success of the course depends upon the responsiveness and outside preparation of each student . . . class discussions will center on those aspects of each play that prove to be the chief interest to the class."

To facilitate this process, early in the semester I provide a list of sample discussion questions for the students. This provides them with some direction as they develop a sense of how to read a play and confidence in their abilities as amateur dramaturgs. As the semester progresses, I eventually stop giving the students handouts because they no longer need them. They have learned to set the agenda for class discussion, and the plays they are reading come to life for them in an immediate and relevant way.

I have also learned to be flexible and respond to the needs of my students. In my film aesthetics course last January, I scheduled *Grand Illusion* and *The Bridge on the River Kwai* for screenings, the first to illustrate principles related to composition, the latter as an example of epic as genre. The Persian Gulf War completely changed my planned lecture / discussion strategies. As a result, I had two of the most exciting class discussions in my experience as a teacher. Students were too overwhelmed by the dissonance they were feeling over the war to engage in any consideration of genre or "mis-en-scene." They were confronting a catastrophic human event and trying to reconcile its appropriateness within the context of their own values. It was a painful experience in which to participate, but the students' insights were a revelation to me because they came from their unique and authentic experience. Their encounters with these two works of film art were astounding, and I would gladly sacrifice content to a growth experience of that proportion. Those class days will be memorable to the students because life and learning became one and the same. We, as teachers, can learn from these exceptional moments as we attempt to move our classrooms daily from content specificity to opening our students' eyes to a broader perspective which will prepare them for life. Oscar Wilde once wrote, "The value of an education lies in what we will remember long after the specifics of what we have been taught have been forgotten." Despite his reputation for sarcasm, Wilde's words seem especially appropriate in today's educational climate.

During the materialism-centered society of the 1980s, liberal arts institutions scrambled to justify their existence. The college and university have come to be perceived by many as a consumer marketplace, where the end goal of the higher education experience is a high paying job. We, as educators, must continue to resist this mentality. The medieval tradition of the liberal arts was based on a humanistic philosophy that sought to foster not only academic development in a specific discipline, but to teach the skills of integration and synthesis, and to develop a personal set of values that would lead to a stronger sense of social responsibility. In today's global community, the liberal arts philosophy is needed more than ever before. It is in this area of our curriculum that our best teaching must take place. If we are to prepare our students for participation in an information-centered, technological society, in which they will have to be retrained numerous times, then their ability to think critically, problem-solve, analyze and synthesize becomes paramount. As Oscar Wilde's words so prophetically suggested, the specific content of our disciplines will often be outdated before our students leave our institutions. We must be dedicated to preparing them for life-long learning if they are to be contributing and responsible members of the global community to which they will belong.

In my senior seminar course, I find, as do many of my colleagues, students making syntheses and integration across the disciplines. *The Bacchae by* Euripides can be studied not just as an example of Greek tragedy with its ritualistic traditions, but as a search for understanding the human condition, such as the balance between the rational and irrational aspects of the human psyche.

When my students study the plays of Henrik Ibsen and the realistic style of playwriting at the end of the nineteenth century, our focus is not only on the theatrical perspective but the broader world view that includes the impact on all avenues of human interaction, of the American and French Revolutions, the industrial and scientific revolutions, and the revolutionary thought of Charles Darwin and Auguste Comte. It is in this integration that students are provided not only with an appreciation of the historic traditions of their culture, but a context for the basic knowledge in their discipline. We must constantly remind them that this base of knowledge is not just facts, but human beings attempting to find truth within the social, political, economic and aesthetic movements of their time.

If we, as educators, are to prepare our students for the difficult challenges of the twenty-first century, if we expect them to act on their civic and global responsibilities, to contribute to the solutions of problems now facing our world, then our most important mandate becomes the formulation of a personal set of values in each of them. We must teach them to make judgments consistent with their values and to modify that system of values as they gain new knowledge and insights from their actions and the actions of their fellow human beings. This is the true challenge of teaching within the liberal arts context and the one to which we must dedicate ourselves.

Reflections on Successful Teaching—Teaching as a Pilgrimage

Mary Ball (Biology)
Carson-Newman College

In one of George Bernard Shaw's plays a character says, "I am not a teacher. I am but a fellow traveler of whom you asked the way. I pointed ahead, ahead of myself as well as of you."

Perhaps the image of "fellow traveler" appeals to me because of my experience with science as a way of knowing rather than as known facts. Perhaps I take solace in the image because it frees me from the need to feel that I am an expert at what I do. Perhaps I find excitement in anticipating the possibilities that may lie ahead. In any case, extension of the metaphor suggests that, just as there is seldom only one road leading to a given destination, there are likely to be numerous paths to successful teaching.

In the dozen or more years that have passed since I first read Shaw's quotation, my own pilgrimage has led me to a liberal arts college, after eleven years as a faculty member at a large, state land-grant university. (While there, I came to refer to it as a "multi-versity" rather than as a university because there was so little integration among the numerous majors and programs.) My experience has been a rewarding one and has convinced me that those of us who teach science at liberal arts colleges have a special opportunity to encourage students to become lifelong learners. The greatest compliment a former student could ever give me would be to say, "You helped me learn how to think more complexly, showed me how exciting new ideas can be, and encouraged me along the way."

Choosing Your Destination

Success involves accomplishing something planned or attempted. Thus, if you know what you want to accomplish and know how to accomplish it, then success ought to be achievable, although measuring it may be difficult; but what should we as teachers be trying to accomplish and how can we find the means?

In describing his pilgrimage as a teacher, a colleague of mine once said, "I started out teaching English, but I came to realize that teaching students is more important." That remark strikes me as being a key to successful teaching: focusing on students rather than on subject matter, setting goals that transcend subject matter. The goal I find most compelling is that of promoting student development.

Promoting Student Development

Through his interviews with Harvard students, William Perry came to see a predictable series of stages through which students pass, although at different rates.[1] Perry did not initially believe that his observations could be used to promote change, but he concluded that change would be desirable because people in the early stages of development tend to be intolerant, while those who function at a higher stage are tolerant of differing viewpoints.

When I attended a seminar on The Perry Scheme, I expected to get some useful tips on helping young people make a career choice. Instead, I heard Perry's associate argue persuasively for the premise that course content matters only in so far as it offers an excuse for teacher and students to interact in ways that promote change in one's ways of thinking about the world. Becoming introduced to Perry's ideas was a turning point for me.

Furthermore, Nevitt Sanford postulated that change requires "challenges" and that appropriate challenges can promote change when balanced with appropriate "supports." For example, establishing rapport with a student may help offset his or her feeling of being threatened when asked to justify a position on an issue. In a seminar presentation entitled "Sharing in the Cost of Growth," Perry pointed out an important caveat to teachers: since changing is often painful, we must be willing to give emotional support if we attempt to stimulate change. In addition to extrinsic support, however, it is important to cultivate intrinsic sources of support that can "keep us going when things get tough."

The Joy of "Aha!" Experiences

The story is told that Archimedes' realization that he could use water displacement to judge the purity of gold in the king's crown came to Archimedes while bathing. The insight is said to have created such euphoria that he ran (naked) through the streets shouting, "Eureka!" ("I have found it!"). In my own experience, the insight which triggers that euphoric feeling sometimes comes so suddenly that I too have felt like shouting "Eureka!" I've never had a student shout "Eureka!" in class, but I have had some interject "Aha!" or "Oh, I see now!" More often, I have observed a sudden look in their eyes, like a light switching on, which conveys "Now I get it!" I counsel students to recall past "Aha!" experiences during times when it seems that the struggle to comprehend is hopeless. Insight may be surprisingly close at hand!

On other occasions insight and the euphoria it generates increase gradually over a period of time in which a new idea is examined and reflected upon. I read *Flatland* as a student in junior high school, but even though 30 years have passed, I can still remember the joy and excitement of that early encounter with the notion that what seems real or true may depend on one's viewpoint.

Historically, scientific inquiry has provided rich opportunities for "Aha!" experiences. Many important scientific insights have occurred to people for whom science was a hobby rather than a profession. Beatrix Potter, of Peter Rabbit fame, was first to realize that plant-like lichens are actually a partnership between an alga and a fungus. Mendel, the Father of Genetics, was a clergyman. Numerous persons from all walks of life have enjoyed pursuing interests in astronomy, botany, and zoology. Among professional scientists, the joy and excitement of scientific inquiry must be a significant motivation for continued dedication to their work. Unfortunately, the style of many research journals makes it impossible for the casual reader to perceive any excitement on the part of the authors.

When I began teaching at the college level, just about any introductory biology textbook described in some detail elegant experiments with *Acetabularia,* a large (up to two inches in length) single-celled, marine alga commonly called "Mermaid's Wineglass." From the results of these experiments, students could easily see that the nucleus well deserves to be described as the "control center of the cell."

Texts of this vintage also were likely to describe many other classic studies from which our current understanding of biology has come. In contrast, current texts define the nucleus as the cell's control center, rather than building a case for that conclusion. Why the change? My guess is that the explosion of new knowledge made it attractive to abandon the old approach in order to cover more and more information. In the process, have we destroyed the atmosphere likely to attract students to science as a profession or to promote a love of science among laypersons?

On Strike Zones and Late Bloomers

Our division chairman occasionally asks the rhetorical question, "Are we pitching too high in our introductory science courses (for majors)?" The usual faculty response it to reject the metaphor and to discourse on the importance of maintaining standards. We might gain some valuable insights by pursuing the metaphor?

Baseball is considered to be a wholesome sport which teaches teamwork and fair play. The notion of the "strike zone" and the need for the impartial perspective of the umpire are important. Although batting .400 is considered a noteworthy achievement at the professional level, in our community, as in numerous others, kids play T-Ball, a variation of baseball designed to let novices be successful in batting. I doubt that the existence of T-Ball is a threat to the quality of major league

48

baseball. If anything, the future of major leagues may depend on the devotion of former T-Ball players who came to love the sport.

Applying the lessons of baseball to teaching science, it seems to me that arranging for novices to be successful and acknowledging each person's "strike zone" (learning style) make good sense. (Science could use more fans among decision-makers, but who would we trust to serve as umpires?) Even if we can't individualize our pitching, perhaps we could be less inclined to call "Strike Three!"

Another metaphor which occurs in our discussions of course content and structure is that of the "late bloomer". Even faculty who reject the strike-zone metaphor are willing to consider the possibility that some of the students who have difficulty in our introductory courses have the potential to succeed, but haven't matured sufficiently. If this view is valid, then we might try to identify late bloomers and have them delay taking certain courses or offer them slower-paced versions of introductory courses.

One advantage of the second metaphor is that we as teachers can't be blamed if some students aren't ready for what we have to offer. I do agree that a year or two of maturity can sometimes make a tremendous difference (as a college junior, I found it puzzling that trigonometry had seemed so difficult two years earlier), but what if the more important cause of students having difficulty is variation in learning styles? Besides providing appropriate challenges and supports and creating opportunities for "Aha!" experiences, how might we take learning styles into account?

Several years ago, my own daughter signed up for my Genetics course. One evening as we were discussing a recent lecture of mine on bacterial conjugation, transduction, and transformation (ways that bacteria can swap genes), she muttered, "What are bacteria good for, anyway?" That one question led to a good deal of soul-searching on my part, and I vowed to give an overview of the importance of bacteria in future semesters.

Does not a teacher have a responsibility to help students create a context for learning new material? What I've read on learning styles theory seems to indicate that some students, for example the "feeling" types on the Myers-Briggs Type Indicator, require context and may not be able to learn without it.[2] Furthermore, those students who appear to be able to learn material without context may be relying on short-term memory.

I fear that that is precisely what is happening in the typical introductory science course. Students who can't learn without context end up changing to a major more obviously relevant to their lives, and students who can rely on short-term memory move on to advanced science courses lacking any real understanding of science concepts. My own decision has been to give context-building a high priority in my teaching, especially in my non-majors classes, where "feeling" types predominate.

Zoology for Non-Majors: A Success Story

When I came to Carson-Newman College in 1985 I found that in the atmosphere of this liberal arts college I had more freedom to explore the application of innovative modes of instruction. I was particularly impressed by the existence of "May Term," a three-week session which historically had emphasized experiential innovative courses. In 1988, I designed a new course to be taught in May Term, called Zoology for Non-Majors. Enrollment was originally limited to ten to maximize student interactions and access to laboratory equipment. After the first year, demand for the course justified our offering two sections, referred to as "tribes," with a colleague and me sharing responsibility for working with 20 students.

Meeting three hours a day for three weeks, students perform "hands-on" laboratory activities, plan and carry out group projects, and present oral reports to members of their own tribe. The students read David Attenborough's book *Life on Earth* and complete worksheets in which they are asked questions designed to test their reading comprehension and to encourage analysis and synthesis. In lieu of lectures and exams, students submit lab reports, a library research paper, and a "Naturalist's Notebook" containing sketches and observations of the organisms present in finger-bowl "mini-ponds."

The course has been enthusiastically praised by students, and I have been consistently impressed by the quality of their work. Group Projects have included building bluebird houses, "landscaping for wildlife" adjacent to the science building, and repairing a 30-gallon aquarium to create a "Crawdad Habitat." Students serve as their own tour guides on a Nature Trail hike in the Smokies, learn techniques of stream-monitoring at a nearby stream, and develop a "Zoo Checklist" to use to evaluate the Knoxville Zoo on our field trip. Laboratory exercises focus on living organisms including goldfish, mealworms, snails, earthworms, and crayfish. Students are given wide latitude in selection of topics for their oral reports. Past topics have included "The Economic Value of Wildlife," "Animals of the Bible," and "The Significance of Honeybees to Humans."

An Agenda for Action

While working on this manuscript, I reread the 1990 report of the American Association for the Advancement of Science (AAAS) Project on Liberal Education and the Sciences, one of many recent publications calling for national educational reform.[3] The report is of particular interest to me because its recommendations are addressed primarily to natural science faculty. This emphasis is justified by the Study Group on the grounds that those of us who teach natural science at the undergraduate level are in a unique position to effect reform through influencing future civic leaders and K–12 teachers.

The report's recommendations are based on two main principles: that science should be taught as a liberal art in all science courses (whether for majors or non-majors) and that science should be taught as it is practiced in order for all students to become scientifically literate, liberally-educated citizens. As the report acknowledges, reform will require major changes in the format of national tests such as the ACT, GRE, and MCAT; abandonment of traditional emphases on survey courses and on "coverage"; effective collaboration between natural science faculty and faculty in the social sciences and humanities; and institutional leadership and support.

Pedagogical Strategies Worth Exploring

To achieve the needed pedagogical shift, the AAAS Study Group urges natural science faculty to "become conversant with research on how people learn science and integrate that knowledge in their science teaching." I am gratified that many of the Study Group's suggestions for improving college science teaching (such as making the study of science meaningful to students from the start; encouraging curiosity about natural phenomena; and including the history, philosophy, and sociology of science and technology in all science classes) are in accord with my own educational philosophy. Suggested pedagogical strategies include group discussion and group projects; student-designed laboratory experiments; and role-playing, writing activities, and diverse assessment methods, all of which I have found to be very useful.

Bernice McCarthy's 4MAT System has been very thought-provoking to me in the last year and I recommend it as a basis for course planning.[4] This instructional model is based on consideration of individual learning styles and provision for both right-brain and left-brain modes of instruction. Following the model, activities are planned to move through an ordered sequence of four "quadrants" of the 4MAT cycle. The developer feels this process is crucial to adequately meet the needs of each of four basic types of learners and to help each learner develop skills representative of the other three types.

This spring, I undertook a revision of the "lecture" component of my sections of our Environmental Science for Non-Majors course using the 4MAT System. In the past I had given lectures on material assigned in the textbook, along with three one-hour short-answer exams and a comprehensive final. A journal and a written critique of an article from *Smithsonian* or *National Geographic* were also required.

Although traditional lecturing can be included in the 4MAT System, I vowed to avoid it as much as possible. Instead, I divided each class of 50 students into permanent groups of from six to eight and emphasized student involvement in class activities. Videotapes were used to set the stage for discussion of issues such as tropical deforestation and global warming. One of the most successful activities was a mock public hearing held to debate the proposal of a connector highway through a wetland (based on the Huntley Meadows controversy). Groups were assigned to represent the Save the Wetlands citizen group, the Lockheed Connector supporters, the National Park

Service, etc. After a short presentation by each group, individuals were allowed time to express their opinions, alternating between the "pro" and "con" sides. One student testified as "Freddy the Frog," squatting on the demonstration table at the front of the classroom and bulging her eyes!

The student reactions I observed during the semester have encouraged me to dream about what could be achieved by expanding the 4MAT approach to all sections of the course and by allowing even more emphasis on "creating personal meaning" and "using knowledge acquired in your own life," the two quadrants of the 4MAT cycle that are most neglected in traditional science courses. I am also excited about the possibility of converting other faculty to consider using the 4MAT System in their courses.

Postscript

I hope the reader will forgive me for spending more time explaining what I'm trying to accomplish in my teaching and why than in giving examples of approaches I have used. I originally intended to stress "what works," as I interpreted my mission as a contributing author. Instead, dear fellow traveler, I've tried to tell you where I'm headed and to encourage you to travel along with me even though I can only point in the general direction of our destination. I challenge you to read the literature on applying the Perry Scheme, on Cooperative Learning, on Writing Across the Curriculum, on Learning Styles, and on the 4MAT System for yourself and to search for your own "Aha!" experiences.[5] Good Luck!

Notes

1. Perry's book contains extensive transcripts of taped interviews with students which illustrate the stages in his model. For an introduction to the model, I recommend that you begin by reading Patricia King's summary of his scheme and the early attempts to apply it. See P. M. King (1978). William Perry's theory of intellectual and ethical development. *Applying New Developmental Findings: New Directions for Student Services, 4,* 35.

2. The Myers-Briggs Type Indicator is routinely administered to incoming freshmen in many colleges.

3. The AAAS Report, *The Liberal Art of Science: Agenda for Action*, is available from AAAS Books, Dept. LES, P.O. Box 753, Waldorf, MD 20604.

4. McCarthy, B. (1987). *The 4MAT System: Teaching to learning styles with right/left mode techniques.* Barrington, IL: Excel, Inc.

5. For an introduction to the Writing Across the Curriculum movement, see *Teaching writing in all disciplines* (1982). *New directions for teaching and learning,* 4. For information on Cooperative Learning, see D. Johnson, R. Johnson, E. Johnson Holubec, and P. Roy (1986). *Circles of Learning: Cooperation in the Classroom.* Alexandria, VA: Association for Supervision and Curriculum Development.

Effective Teaching As Practical Wisdom

Bruce Griffith (History)
Catawba College

I can imagine few honors greater than being deemed an effective teacher by respected colleagues, nor can I imagine a greater responsibility than that of offering advice to colleagues with whom I share the honorable but challenging task of educating young American adults for the twenty-first century. This honor and challenge is increased when the audience is composed primarily of those who bear responsibility for the development of teachers, for whatever effect an educator may have is thereby multiplied.

Accused of corrupting the youth of Athens, Socrates stressed a point we must all recall: teachers must live in the community in which their students become citizens and thus suffer the consequences of their faulty teaching. If we prepare poor teachers, we multiply the damage we do to ourselves and others.

If I am to comment on effective teaching, certainly I should be able to define what is meant by "effective." Many of us would begin with a utilitarian definition of effective teaching as that which promotes the greatest increase in learning for the greatest number of students. Certainly one cannot describe teaching as effective if students fail to learn; but every educator who has ever been connected even remotely with the debate over evaluation is aware of the difficulties of assuming any simple causal connection between good teaching and measurable gains in learning. Are low levels of student advancement in inner city schools due to poor teachers? Is a teacher effective if he or she promotes slightly more learning by the majority of average students but fails to motivate the academically gifted minority to achieve their potential? Is improved performance on standardized tests an accurate measure of the sort of learning that is the goal of higher education? The utilitarian calculus of greatest total benefit is no simple matter in education; but if we cannot agree on how to measure effective teaching, how can we hope to promote it?

One response to the recognition that even good teaching may not always produce learning is to focus on technique or method. The assumption underlying this approach is that teaching is in some sense a science, or that it resembles engineering. When the underlying psychological principles governing learning are understood and applied skillfully, teaching is effective. If students obstinately refuse to learn from an effective teacher, some external factor must be responsible. In this model good teaching involves teacher behavior and can be measured without reference to student learning.

Most of those who teach at the post-secondary level reject the notion that they should be "engineers of the mind," as Joseph Stalin imagined them to be. Rather, they either consider effective teaching to consist exclusively of the mastery and clear presentation of content or to be a gift or an art. The first assumption divorces the measurement of effective teaching from student learning, for one's expertise in a discipline can only be measured by others in that field, and the possession of the doctorate is a certification of such expertise. The vision of teaching as an art or a gift, on the other hand, is student-centered, but it denies that any sort of training can produce an effective teacher. Those who are effective are so because, like great artists, their inner beings are fully expressed in the art of teaching. Such gifted teachers utilize with skill many of the techniques identified by researchers as effective, but they do so in an organic and intuitive or natural way.

It must be very confusing for our future teachers to learn that certain methodologies are essential to good teaching and then, in the next period, to observe a professor who violates virtually all of those methodological principles. If, as is often the case, this "bad" teacher is able to promote learning in students, the confusion increases. Nor is this an exceptional instance. On the average, if effective teaching is measured by student learning, post-secondary educators are more effective than those at the secondary level, though they are in most cases virtually untrained in teaching methodology. The most obvious explanation of this situation, if I am correct, is that we at the college level need to do less to promote learning by our students because those most resistant to learning have left the system before they got to us. Those who go on to college will learn because they are more able and more motivated, so teaching can be more effective as measured by learning, even though it may be less skilled.

Many of my colleagues betray this assumption as they complain about lower admissions standards and being forced to teach lower-level courses for non-majors. Overtly and indirectly all of us have been exposed in our graduate training to the premise that the scholar is superior to the mere teacher, and that insofar as teaching is rewarding it resembles the graduate seminar in which independent learners, having mastered the methodology of the discipline, present and critique each other's potential contributions to the expansion of human knowledge. Effective teaching in this model can only be expected in upper-level courses for majors in reasonably selective institutions. Such classes are necessarily small, so the measure of effective teaching is qualitative rather than quantitative.

But what of the masses? What of the required freshman survey class in which one is expected to produce learning by large numbers of students whose prior knowledge and motivation is suspect and whose disciplinary preparation is almost certainly inadequate? University professors by their behavior generally demonstrate their disdain for such courses, but by a process of self-selection considerable numbers of teachers who welcome this challenge end up at small liberal arts colleges. I consider myself to be one of these.

Admittedly the freshman-level General Education course is a challenge, but it seems to me to be the most fascinating a college teacher can meet. The "cafeteria style" curricula of the 1970's and early 1980's assured that most of us did not have to face this challenge squarely, but as we have returned to some sort of core, more and more of us do and will. We should welcome it as an opportunity to grow as teachers, but we must realize that our fullest utilization of that opportunity requires that we collaborate. I would like to believe that after more than twenty-five years of teaching, I am not only effective but more effective than I was a decade ago. If so, I owe this to those who have helped me in my effort to learn to teach better: my colleagues.

The contrasting models of effective teaching I have described are all, in a sense, myths. Each is based upon one or more fundamental truths and helps to clarify some dimension of teaching and learning. Teaching well requires both the discipline of science and the creativity of art, but it demands even more. The Greeks, as usual, had a word for it—*phronesis*. This term is translated in various ways; but its essence is captured in the term "practical wisdom" or, more simply, "good sense." They used the term *techne* to describe the ability to do or make something well, while phronesis was the wisdom to live well. It was learned not from books but from living. The great playwrights of the Golden Age of Athens frequently centered their tragedies on the consequences of a lack of practical wisdom, as in Sophocles's *Oedipus Rex* and *Antigone*. Thucydides equally valued this quality, which required that individuals or communities recognize the importance of the decision to be made and deliberate with the care demanded by that importance.

Greek writers from Homer to Aristotle recognized that phronesis might be a gift found even in a young person, but more often it was the product of the experience of living. A long life, however, was no guarantee of wisdom. Phronesis was most likely to develop when the individual habitually sought advice from others. The sort of decisions which demand practical wisdom are those which involve what problem-solving schema define as "ill-formed problems" because the rules for reaching a solution are not clear and because they can be made only once. It stands to reason that the broader the experience brought to bear on the decision, the less likely individual weaknesses will lead to an unwise decision. Pericles, in his famous funeral oration, argued forcefully that Athens was wiser than her rivals because all of her citizens participated in the process of decision-making. Further, he insisted that Athenians were individually wiser because of their participation in this process.

If the Greeks recognized the value of collaboration in the solution of complex human problems, why have we in higher education ignored it? In recent years many of us have become convinced that it is an effective technique for promoting student learning, yet we use it rarely ourselves in our effort to solve the complex and very important problem of promoting learning among a diverse group of young adults. We collaborate in designing our curricula, but we make our decisions as teachers of particular courses as isolated individuals.

Perhaps the reason is that many of us identify ourselves with our disciplines rather than seeing ourselves as educators. As specialists we seem to have little to discuss with colleagues, unless perhaps they are in our discipline, and even in this latter case our individualism and assignment to different courses limits sharing. If, however, practical wisdom is an essential quality for effective teaching, programs can be designed to promote the collaboration which will foster it. It is to such a program that I owe what I hope is an increase in my effectiveness.

Catawba's freshman program is year-long, interdisciplinary, and required of all students. Its content focuses primarily on what selected ancient civilizations thought about the appropriate goals for humans individually and collectively. Much of the emphasis of the program, however, is on developing college-level cognitive abilities and easing the affective stresses of the transition into college life. More than a third of our faculty are involved as lecturers, composition instructors, or master learners (freshman advisors and small group mentors). We have collectively shaped every part of the program including the design of the text, shared lecture outlines, examinations, exercises, and discussion topics. We have found that this design process, which substantially limits the nearly absolute freedom enjoyed by most college professors, actually enhances our individual skills and creativity.

I have found, for example, that dialogue with teachers whose discipline, age, or learning style is radically different from mine has been of enormous value in helping me understand those of my students who are unlike me. Furthermore, I have learned techniques not natural to my own style which are effective in engaging such students in the learning process. I am constantly forced to think carefully about my objectives and to be able to justify every activity designed for the students in our program. If I omit a transition in a lecture, one of our master learners will point this out to me. An ambiguous objective question rarely escapes notice, and essay questions appear on examinations only after their designers have carefully described the parameters of a good response. When students are confused, we know it immediately, rather than after they have failed graded work.

Admittedly this program is highly labor-intensive, and the egos of program faculty are often bruised in the frankly critical atmosphere of our collaboration. The benefits, however, far outweigh the costs. Our students are treated more fairly than might otherwise be the case, and their multiple contacts with faculty in the program allow us to diagnose their individual difficulties more quickly and accurately than we could in isolation. In the program we see ourselves as educators first and disciplinary experts second, and we carry some of that identification into our more specialized courses for majors. In short, we are wiser and therefore more effective teachers.

The advantages of such a program for students who are beginning their training to be teachers should be evident. Every teacher is shaped as much by concrete models of effective teaching as by educational theory. A program designed to clarify expectations and to help students meet them is an ideal model for those who are preparing to teach. Furthermore, for these young people who will soon be attempting to solve the decidedly ill-formed problems posed daily to those teaching in the public schools, such a program can be a model of how educators should cooperate, demonstrate mutual respect while arguing vigorously, and generally deliberate well about the supremely important issues of the ends and means of education.

Our education faculty assure me that they can see a significant and positive difference in the students who have gone through our program as freshmen. I can see an equally significant and positive difference in myself and my colleagues in the program. Our shared ultimate goals are clearer, our skills as teachers are expanded and sharpened, and our ability to choose the effective means to accomplish our noble purpose —our phronesis or practical wisdom—has been greatly enhanced.

Taking Account of the Personal in Teaching

Rose Marie Hurrell (Psychology)
College of New Rochelle

The personal is the storehouse which supplies the food-stuff of my teaching. It is the source which gives character to my teaching, the nutriment which supports it, and the reserve that replenishes it. I draw from it to inquire, to instruct, to refute, and to corroborate. While my training as a psychologist gives bent to my teaching, my style, technique and method have been adopted to suit me, the person, rather than me, the professional. My ideas about what teaching is, my beliefs about what good teachers do, and the way that I conduct myself as a teacher arise from my personal experience with learning and with the people who are a part of that experience.

Learning has always had special appeal for me. That I came to appreciate and enjoy it very early in my life was due largely to my father, who held me intellectually captivated as a child and even as an adult with his gifts for storytelling and humor. Like *Aesop's fables*, his tales were masterfully crafted lessons that often provoked consternation in me and always caused me to ponder and reflect. Every childish question I posed represented an opportunity for him to tease or assuage my curiosity. He never missed a chance to inject the wisdom of his humor into my education, often using it as balm to medicate and revive my sometimes weary and frustrated resolve. For the two of us, learning was merriment made meaningful as we frolicked together as partners in play. Under his tutelage I learned eagerly and lovingly. I embraced learning for all that it brought me but understood its importance to my life only in an immature way.

It was not until adolescence that I became passionate about learning and its promise to mystify and reveal. I pursued it ardently and, for the first time, awkwardly. What was a straightforward and simple process became vague and burdened with complexity. The naive certainty that carried me so willingly into intellectual entanglements as a child gave way to self-conscious concerns and anxieties. The sense of abandon that freed me to examine without inhibition evaporated, leaving behind only a trace of the uninhibited. My relationship to learning was transformed from one of carefree engagement to one of guarded solicitude.

Maturity eased the tentativity and self-protectiveness of adolescence and brought with it a need for self-expansion and personal fulfillment that intensified my involvement in learning. With the intellectual discipline that accompanies age, learning took direction and form, and expressed itself as a lifelong commitment to teaching.

Like my father, I believe that to teach is to participate as a partner in learning. This participation entails more than a contract to instruct and inform. It requires of the teacher a commitment to provide, support, and protect. It makes of the teacher a comrade who cooperates in the learning transaction and a beneficiary who shares in its profits.

Good teaching is born of an appreciation of the complexity of learning and of the people taking part in it. Good teachers know what abilities, skills and deficiencies their students bring to the learning situation. More characteristically, they know their students beyond the requirements of learning. They know them as individual personalities with interests, attitudes, and habits that can fortify or demean learning. Good teachers know their students as persons with lives outside of the classroom and they use their knowledge of the personal to give learning relevance and meaning.

In my years of teaching, I have come to rely increasingly on the power of the personal to arouse interest and ignite discussion. I will, for example, begin a class by asking students to write an answer to a question that relates to their personal experience and that will serve as the basis for discussion and analysis. In Adolescent Psychology, a favorite question of mine is, "What color was your adolescence?" The responses are as personal as they are varied, and when students are then asked to tell why they chose their particular color, the backdrop for an exploration of the nature of the adolescent experience is set in place. Students are pressed into careful reflection and analysis as they are forced to consider how factors such as race, gender, ethnicity, and class contribute to their own and others' experience. Without fail, the exercise results in an intensely involving dialogue that expands the limited understanding which readings or lectures impart.

When students come to me in desperation for guidance in selecting a research topic or project, I point them to their own interests or extracurricular activities as possibilities. The result is often far more fruitful than if I handed them a menu of viable but, from their point of view, boring topics. Their work has relevance, takes on more vitality, and progresses less tediously when the personal is given expression and validity within the academic.

Beyond a knowledge of students, good teaching requires an appreciation of the importance of environment to learning and an understanding of the kind of environment which promotes successful learning. For me, the essence of such an environment is affective. It is one in which feelings of trust, respect, acceptance, and worthiness serve as the platform for learning and where honest effort, imaginative thinking, intellectual curiosity, and individual initiative are prized and rewarded.

As a teacher, I work a great deal on building trust. Trust is the substance which invisibly draws student and teacher together as they venture into the domain of intellectual discovery. It permits each the freedom to engage in learning untethered by the fear of intimidation or embarrassment. It supports, maintains, and replenishes learning at every level.

Building trust takes a good deal of time and great care and is more difficult to do as learning becomes more demanding. I see this when I teach the Junior Research Seminar, a psychology course which requires students to produce an original research proposal and to design and lead weekly seminars. Many students enter this course feeling insecure and unwilling to trust themselves and their own capacities to the tasks. I can feel their disbelief and desperation in the very first class meeting as we discuss the course syllabus. From the start, students are apprehensive and skeptical. In some cases, their self-perceived inadequacies create a state of near panic that is semi-paralyzing.

In approaching this situation, I take an aggressively positive position with regard to both the students and the requirements of the course. To obtain support for my position I encourage students to rethink, rework, and revise continually and use the "before and after" products as convincing evidence to bolster and reinforce their self-confidence. I encourage a spirit of cooperation and urge students to serve as resources and supports to one another. I rely on candor, consistency, and conscientious follow-through in my own conduct to gain the confidence of students. To allay the anxiety of uncertainty, I try always to adhere to the details in the course syllabus without deviation, and when change is called for, I negotiate with students to avoid hardship or unpleasant surprises.

One of the most valuable by-products of the weekly seminar meetings is the opportunity they provide me to learn from the students who lead them. When this occurs, the process which students often perceive as unidirectional is reversed as I acquire the status of learner and students step into the role of expert. As our experience converges, feelings meld, ideas and insights surface more freely, and intellectual exchange becomes easier and more fluid.

When I teach, I make it a rule to be myself as much as possible and to give honest expression to the many facets of who I am. I have adopted an informal teaching style which can accommodate the degree of structure mandated by different course content and that provides me with an optimum level of comfort. Because, like many students, I enjoy variety and need change of pace, I use videotapes, demonstrations, group activities, and even games as vehicles to involve and activate students. I am a physically active person and my need for motion takes form in the classroom. When lecturing, I am seldom still, preferring to roam inquisitively about the room. My teaching is accentuated with movement and gesticulation, sometimes unconsciously, sometimes deliberately. I will pose to demonstrate a state of catatonia, trip across the door jam to stage a discussion on attribution theory, and squat and move on all fours to illustrate the kind of abnormal motor development that can sometimes result from early deprivation. Unable to disguise or hide my emotions, I use them to fuel and humanize my teaching.

I have been told by a former student that I am good at what I do because I am "so normal." She got that sense of me I am sure, not from watching me teach expertly, but from observing me struggle, hesitate, and err. She witnessed my moments of quiet grace and comic clumsiness. As my colleague in learning, she was privy to the full range of my humanity, with its strengths and weaknesses exposed. Knowing me in this way provided the basis for the kind of "connecting" that eased our relationship and freed her from its distractions to concentrate exclusively on the business of learning.

In the course of my education, I have been privileged to learn in the company of a handful of excellent college teachers. They came from different disciplines, espoused different philosophies, and favored different pedagogical methods. They differed in style, manner, talents, and personality. One was soft-spoken and eloquent, a second was startlingly dramatic, and a third was surprisingly ingenuous. A teacher of literature had powers to lend music and beauty to the written word while a physicist was peculiarly adept at making the abstract understandable.

Apart from these differences, they had in common important similarities. All were dedicated teachers and scholars whose skills, knowledge, and expertise gained them the respect and credibility of both students and colleagues. They genuinely cared about their students and their presence in the classroom conveyed warmth, enthusiasm, and fairness. Their teaching was infused with a spirit of generosity and dignity that amplified and ennobled it. Each one seemed to enjoy teaching and that enjoyment was matched by a firm conviction in its value.

The example of excellence set by these teachers and others like them is the most important legacy which higher education can bequeath to future teachers. Because it transcends style, method, and technique, excellence speaks to prospective teach-

66

ers of all levels and disciplines. Its universal message contains purpose, influence, and inspiration. Excellence bestows eminence on teaching, assigns distinction to it, and enhances its powers to attract the ablest and most gifted to its fold.

Like scholarship and research, teaching finds its form in the mind and spirit of a single dedicated individual whose training, skills, and talents give rise to its particular quality. To find expression, the quality of excellence needs encouragement and support. To flourish, it requires acknowledgement and reward. The obligation to provide these requisites rests with all who participate in higher education, whether student, teacher, or administrator.

A Note In Your Pocket: What Teachers Do For Students

Laura Winters (English)
College of Saint Elizabeth

Remember the three best teachers you've ever had. Begin to consider what made them good teachers. Remember specific moments in which you reveled in their attention and care.

A good teacher can make each of us feel, if only for a few moments, that we are the most important persons in the world, that it is our duty to act responsibly, that we must always behave in accord with our best selves. The best teachers possess intelligence, wit, a clarity of self-definition, an unmistakable pleasure in watching us learn, a willingness to let us experiment and benefit from successes as well as failures, an understanding that we *will* find our way. The best teachers always keep the faith.

When I was a young person, my older friends would sometimes place hand-written notes in my shirt pockets before I went to what they were afraid might be a wild party: "Remember we value you." "You are the only one of you we've got." "We are responsible for each other." "You are a woman of strong convictions."

Well, the world is a wild party, and we all need those reminders in our shirt pockets. Experience, yes, but remember what is valuable; remember what endures; remember who you are. Our best teachers never let us forget.

Sister Ellen Joyce, a colleague who teaches theology, reminds me often that the fundamental act of justice is to define the self. We need to remind our students that it is their responsibility to accomplish this life-long task. Human beings are meaning-making animals. We all must consciously imagine and create the narratives of our lives, and the teachers we remember best help remind us of that fact.

I teach at a small, liberal arts college for women, and I come to work each day with an expectation of pleasure. My students so frequently delight me that I wonder at the blessing of being a teacher. It often occurs that I have a lecture prepared on a writer or a literary period—my ideas solid and clear—and the first question a student asks forces me to subtly rearrange those notions.

Like Willa Cather's Professor Godfrey St. Peter, in *The Professor's House*, I am a slave to youth and intelligence. An inquisitive mind is a value beyond measure. If the vicissitudes of our lives, the weight of our work loads, and the politics of education make us forget all else, we must recall the pure joy of learning that perhaps led us to teaching in the first place. When asked why he was a painter, a contemporary artist once said, "Because I like the smell of paint." I am a teacher, in part, because I derive continued joy from the details of the classroom. The appearance of back-to-school supplies can still inspire me because I know what is ahead: new books, new ideas, and new students.

I believe my students trust me to create a safe and challenging classroom environment in which they can be bold in their assertions, can make mistakes, and can continue to refine their ideas. Because I teach in a women's college, I am intensely aware that my students often have been valued more for their appearance and their reticence than for their willingness to share their ideas. I feel that it is my task to help my students realize that they are valuable and that only when they begin to respect themselves will they be able to work to help others.

I teach in an institution of good teachers. I am a good teacher in part because my colleagues offer a model for me of flexibility, of commitment, of willingness to spend time with students, of dedication to the life of the mind. Good teachers never work alone. They may sometimes work in opposition to systems which don't value their contributions (and this is a reality we must prepare our students to face), but to be an excellent teacher one must have a community of like-minded people, no matter how small or geographically distant.

Teachers have a responsibility to remember how impressionable some of our students can be. We need to be careful what we impress upon them. One of our most important tasks is to convey our enthusiasm for our subject. We want our students to fall in love with ideas, as we have.

Because my own specialty is twentieth century literature, I believe that modernist and contemporary art is especially well suited to suggest the value of subtlety, the subjectivity of human experience, the role of irony, and the need for active responsibility in coming to terms with a work of art and with our own lives. The audience of modernist art must actively participate in the creation of meaning. Consider Marcel Duchamp's "Nude Descending a Staircase," Gertrude Stein's *Tender Buttons*, and Virginia Woolf's *To the Lighthouse*. The audience must piece together bits, scraps of conversation, or geometrical forms in order to create a coherent whole. Students must understand that writers don't "hide" their meanings. Instead textual complexity results from the choice of a style appropriate to the richness and complexity of human experience. Teachers need an appreciation of figures of speech, particularly irony, which they may one day find helpful in their chosen fields.

Teachers must know how to write and how to teach their students how to write. I believe that every student who graduates with a degree in teacher education ought to have a course in writing theory and pedagogy, taught by an expert in those fields. The writing classroom is particularly well suited to teacher education. It is impossible to run a successful writing classroom that does not include active participation by all of its members. One can only speak about writing theoretically for so long. Think of a swimming class without access to a pool. No go. The student in the writing classroom must focus, organize, and develop ideas. She/he must be aware of the needs of the audience, and must learn that it is the mark of the good writer to learn what to save and what to discard or put aside for future use. The perfect metaphor in the wrong place is no help at all. In the writing classroom we learn by painful and exhilarating experience that every work written is the result of a series of conscious choices on the part of the writer.

Each teacher should also take a course in which she/he comes to terms with the creation of the visual image. As we move into the twenty-first century, our students will be as influenced by the visual as they are by the written word. It is a waste of time to bemoan this fact; we must address it, learn how to harness its power, and hope that our love of literature will in small and large ways serve as a model for our students.

Most important, I think, every teacher must have a solid base of information and experience within an academic field in order to possess some basis from which to speak with students. This is not merely an option. It is perhaps the most vital part of a student's education, and departments of teacher education must continue to make this clear in their statements of purpose, their scheduling practices, and in their conversations with students.

I will say it simply. There is nothing more important in the formulation of excellent teachers than excellent teaching. We may remember information; we may remember courses, but there are teachers we can never forget. Liberal arts colleges must foster an atmosphere in which good teaching is discussed (by students and teachers alike) and rewarded. Students who wish to become teachers must see that the profession of teaching is valued by their own professors, by administrators, by parents, and by the culture at large. As teachers, we are all responsible to shift public opinion on matters pertaining to education by our words and by our example.

In *A Room of One's Own*, Virginia Woolf suggests that in order to write fiction, a woman needs an independent income and a room of her own. I suggest that every teacher needs at least a figurative, if not a literal, room of her own, a place to step into in order to judge her progress, to regroup, to evaluate options, and to work. In the same way we videotape teachers to show them the strengths and weaknesses of their self-presentation, a student of teacher education must develop an internal videotape ability in which she constantly refines her own ideas about teaching.

In *Parallel Lives*, a wonderful biographical portrait of five Victorian marriages and a poetic meditation on the politics of human relations, Phyllis Rose defines love as "the momentary or prolonged refusal to think of another person in terms of power." As a teacher I often call upon that definition when dealing with my students in and out of the classroom. If we are tempted to judge our students harshly when they don't perform as we'd like, we must remember that we can never know fully what they have been through in their lives. We must be aware that students from backgrounds and cultures other than our own may be interpreting our words very differently than we are meaning them.

We must love our students, according to Rose's definition.

We must always be aware of the power of teachers. Because I believe that teaching can reinforce the worst aspects of the desire for control inherent in the human condition, we teachers must always look critically at the ways we exercise power. Learning ought to liberate our students, for it certainly will form them.

Pursuing a Heritage

Robert McJimsey (History)
Colorado College

L iberal learning contains a definable heritage of which we academics are trustees. That heritage came to fruition in Europe between 1500 and 1800. It sprang from two founding principles. First, liberal learning catered to the whole person, emphasizing that versatility was the handmaiden of success. Second, it freed the laity from the authority of that specialized, institutional learning characteristic of the Middle Ages. Liberal learning joined reforming elements within Christianity to link the study of ancient and biblical texts to the maturation of moral responsibility. By 1800 it had added a concern with science and utility, producing general curricula of study in the form of encyclopedias of knowledge. Throughout these and subsequent adaptations liberal education has remained true to its founding principles. It honors versatility by offering the student a variety of subjects and by giving each student a generous latitude of choice. And it remains skeptical of dogmas, of absolutes, and of specialized training.

The period between 1500 and 1800 also recognized a variety of arrangements for the presentation of that learning which was worthy of human freedom. Castiglione's circle of friends at Urbino constructed the perfect courtier. Montaigne's essays and Erasmus' Colloquies illustrated the personal and social importance of learning. In the eighteenth century the salon and the literary club became models of informed conversation. Attributes of these models of polite society gradually found their way into the classroom. Lectures were to be pleasing as well as informative; discussion was welcomed and tutorials idealized; field trips and study abroad were prized.

Sustaining this heritage has long been the mission of the liberal arts college. Rather than prescribe a "customary" form of instruction most colleges give teachers latitude to experiment, to work out a strategy and a style. My own teaching has evolved from stand-up lectures, to a mixture of lecture-cum-recitation to my present format in which students take the lead. I begin class by handing out questions based on the day's assignment. Usually I give two students the same question and ask them to work together on its answer. After a break of about ten minutes, the class reconvenes and each group makes an extemporaneous presentation of its answer. A general discussion and my own comments follow each presentation. The questions themselves are framed in relation to the character of the assigned readings. Readings from textbooks elicit composite questions: "Use Greek literature, philosophy and art to construct the goals of Greek life." Scholarly books draw out questions bent toward analysis: "What was revolutionary about Cromwell's New Model Army?" Readings from primary sources often ask for a more reflective response: "Does Peter Abelard's autobiography show him to have strong religious convictions?" Other questions may call for more straightforward description. Depending on the breadth of the questions and the depth of responses, a class meeting of about ninety minutes can absorb five to eight presentations.

When the size of the class is fifteen or fewer, I employ a tutorial format. After one or two sessions discussing the reading, students meet with me in groups of three to read essays they have written to one another. Together we discuss each essay's form and content. Student response to both of these formats has been positive. I tell the class that there will be no "wallflowers," and commonly the students tell me how much they value being given the opportunity to lead off a discussion.

The students learn each system quickly and have little trouble organizing their extemporaneous presentations. They soon realize that someone who has not prepared the assignment ahead of time will make a dull, repetitious showing. For each of these formats it is fairly easy to evaluate class participation, and even to base a percentage of each student's final

74

mark on that participation. Evaluation of work done is also a full part of liberal education. From Erasmus to Voltaire and beyond scholars have engaged in correspondence redefining, explaining, and defending their ideas. All of these scholars presented themselves as masters of their civilization's learning, and they were continually held to account for their claims. The conversation of the classroom is part of this evaluation. That conversation also flows into more prosaic forms of examination. Usually my students take examinations composed of a section of short answer questions keyed to material covered in their extemporaneous presentations, and a section of discussion questions. At the last instructional meeting the students submit their own evaluations of the course.

Cooperative teaching attests to the versatility of liberal learning. Every year I teach with at least two colleagues, usually in political science, English literature, or art history. Few, if any subjects are impervious to a shared format. For instance, each year six faculty members offer to our first year students a course on the Renaissance, covering three units (one unit lasting three and one-half weeks). Each unit is co-taught by two faculty members representing different disciplines. Over the past three years history, romance languages, religion, political philosophy, English literature, art history, music, and physics have furnished participants.

Twenty years ago, at this course's inception, we were very much our own first year students, wondering how the course would work out. During that first year, instructors pressed their own versions of the Renaissance. By the second year, a few dominant themes had surfaced: the antimonies of appearance and reality, the inner and the outer self, ceritas and cupiditas, the institutional and the personal. After that the main questions became administrative. Who would pair with whom? What readings could be fitted in? Teaching styles and formats varied. Art historians kept to the slide lecture, the physicist took the class on an evening field trip to see in the sky what Galileo saw, while most of us sat around a table conversing over the day's assignment. Usually one teacher at a time was in charge, with the partner in the class acting as a reminder of connections to general themes. As it turned out the only requirement for successful co-teaching was a mildly irenic willingness to find points of contact between our disciplines. For students and instructors the course became a salon of liberal discourse. Year after year, graduates of Renaissance Culture tell how they had continued to refer to the course over their four years. For all of us Renaissance Culture was an introduction to the liberal arts.

All teachers tailor their classes to suit their priorities and their resources. Teachers who by nature want more control over their material will find my own classroom format vexatious. Others may find that my format limits reading assignments too closely to material of a length and complexity suitable for class discussion. There is, moreover, one necessary administrative support for this format of extemporaneous presentations. Colorado College sets a limit of twenty-five students on each of its courses (the daily duration of class is open-ended). Above twenty-five participants, the opportunity to emulate the salon, the literary club, or the circle of friends breaks down. Liberal education will always make substantial claims on human and financial resources. Whether society can afford these ideals is a perennial question.

In addition to reliance on institutional financial resources, faculty members find their mental assets stretched to cover teaching and scholarly obligations. Ideally these two pursuits should nourish one another. The scholarship of Erasmus and his colleagues was prodigious. But they also wished to touch a wider audience, entertaining visions of an educated laity, of ploughmen pausing to sing the psalms. Their efforts supported vernacular languages. Church reformers took up the vernacular, based hymns on folk melodies, and focused worship on the moral edification of the sermon.

For many liberal arts colleges pursuit of these Erasmian ideals has turned into a struggle over the apportionment of resources between teaching and scholarship. Today as class sizes swell to accommodate lighter teaching loads, teaching and scholarship grind against each other. Liberal arts colleges stressing the formal scholarship of peer review and publication cater to the orthodoxies of post graduate education, wedging teaching and scholarship into distinct activities. This trend is unnecessary. The essays, letters, speeches, and treatises of Renaissance scholarship attest to the varieties of scholarly discourse. Today similar avenues for scholarly discourse abound. These include the summer seminar, public lecture, professional newsletter, and professional conferences. There is even a computer-mail network over which historians share their ideas. The communication of our scholarly interests with both peers and public is proper stewardship of our talents. Colleges resisting the crammed classroom and encouraging these many forms of scholarly conversation cultivate the heritage of liberal education.

If versatility and conversation describe the essential content and form of liberal education, what implications do these elements hold for the training of teachers themselves? Some wish to refocus teacher education on the study of Great Books; others urge certification candidates to concentrate on the basic 3-Rs; others recommend that student teachers stress tighter classroom discipline. These critics play upon the suspicion that education programs emphasize "method" at the expense of "content" and favor rewarding a student's "experience" at the expense of rigorous evaluation. Again, the history of liberal education resolves these fears. Between 1500 and 1800 the Humanist interest in classical texts broadened to embrace an expanding vista of human knowledge. Throughout this period form and content marched hand-in-hand, reaching a watershed with the Lockean prescription that kindness, encouragement and other benign forms of psychological management should replace the notorious savagery of the Renaissance schoolmaster. In America this liberal heritage joined the democratic ideal of an educated citizenry to place pedagogy at the center of American education. If the heritage of liberal education were to flourish, teachers would need to know both what it comprised and how to present it to a wider audience.

Teacher education required, therefore, integration into the liberal arts curriculum. It also had to express the liberal arts in terms suitable to the needs and demands of the classroom and the community. The education program at Colorado College testifies to these requirements. No students major in education. Students are screened for admission to the program by a variety of criteria. These criteria stress the students' ability to communicate in written and oral form. Students must write up their observations made during sixty hours of aiding in the local schools. They must submit an essay giving reasons for pursuing a career in teaching. They are interviewed by an ad hoc panel including a classroom teacher. They must receive endorsement from the department in which they are majoring, and they must pass the Basic Skills Screening Test (California Achievement Test and oral English). The certification program mandates courses in the history and philosophy of education as well as courses appropriate to the student's proposed teaching certification. The program addresses the reciprocity between classroom and community with a weekly seminar at which representatives from the local schools discuss communication with parents, classroom management, and school administration. A twelve week practicum in the classroom rounds out each student's certification program. This integration of pedagogy, subject matter, and experience rests upon the cooperation of college administrators, faculty, and department chairs.

The transfer of liberal learning from its Renaissance settings into the classroom not only placed fresh demands upon the teacher, it also forced a review of the basic relationship between teacher and pupil. If liberal education emphasizes the personal and social importance of learning, then excellence in teaching should accentuate the cultivation of affective skills. This prospect opened a vast range of pedagogical possibilities, many of them explored by the experiments of the "progressive education" movement. Today affective learning is undergoing skeptical scrutiny. Amid evidence of grade inflation, slumping test scores, and the paring down of graduation requirements, there are calls to restore institutional responsibility and teacher "authority." Excellence in teaching, it is claimed, should appear in the form of higher scores on achievement tests. Such prescriptions raise the prospect of a turn toward specialization in learning. Teachers should teach what is necessary to pass standardized examinations. "Core" curricula should define a common body of knowledge and should prepare students to assume a particular niche in our complex society. In the pursuit of excellence liberal learning should make way for greater stress on training.

This essay argues that such steps are unnecessary. It is possible to create programs integrating pedagogy and subject matter. It is possible to define excellence in teaching as an appreciation of the heritage of liberal learning, the study of subjects central to that heritage, and the mastery of a pedagogy appropriate to the transmission of that heritage. If we think of the teacher as the trustee of this heritage, we can dispense with much of the quandary surrounding the relationship between teacher and pupil. Teachers are neither servants of particular social and economic agendas, nor are they simply managers of classroom activities. Trustees do not automatically bend to the demands of their beneficiaries (in this case the students). They do not heed the pressures of third parties (social and political action groups). To be effective trustees they require adequate resources and support from their institutions of employment. Institutions which acknowledge and defend this notion of trusteeship will have done a great deal to create the conditions under which the heritage of liberal learning can flourish.

Rather than demand a return to a pre-Renaissance concern with training, our leaders should acknowledge and affirm the value of this heritage. Liberal learning deserves to be carried on because it has been the great answer of western civilization to a time of profound crisis. The transition from the specialization of the Middle Ages to the liberal learning of the Renaissance came about because medieval civilization had fallen into a profound social, political and economic crisis, a crisis which the leading specialists of that time—in Church and State—had failed to resolve. The argument of the period from 1500 to 1800 had been that creativity, productivity, and opportunity were best promoted by an education combining what today are called the humanities, social sciences, and natural sciences. If today we find ourselves threatened by a host of problems, we should seek to renew that heritage which our ancestors designed to meet just such a challenge.

The Teaching Self

Timothy L. Garner (Sociology)
Franklin College

Perhaps one of the most crucial forms of identity we can possess in this culture is that of what we "do for a living." Each occupational category is a socially constructed entity which embodies a complex set of both emergent and institutionalized expectations. These behavioral and attitudinal expectations provide us with symbolically anchored referents through which we can attach meaning to the everyday experiences of self and others. Thus, when one identifies self as "teacher" such a claim operates to evoke a variety of responses (both from audience and presenter) which derive from a collective interpretation of what meanings can and should be attached to such an individual.

An awareness of the existence of manifold interpretations surrounding the cultural form of teacher complicates the picture somewhat as we begin to explore the parameters of our membership in the social world of teaching. The teacher must draw upon the sequence of prior and ongoing life experiences which constitute a unique stock of knowledge in order to establish a sense of identity. Clearly, there are many voices which speak to the teacher in this process of identity formation and maintenance. Some of them provide clarity, while others may obscure or confuse; some are obtrusive discourses on who and what we are, while others are vague whispers that barely permeate our awareness of self. The voices we choose to listen to and give life to in our expressions of self as teacher are crucial and defining components of every action which we engage in as teachers and will determine to a great extent the nature and quality of teaching we can offer to our students.

Who speaks to me and through me as I live out my identity as teacher before that institutionalized form of human grouping that I refer to as "my class"? The most obvious answer is the collective voice of those teachers who have connected with my life in formative ways. I do not wish to conceptually limit this notion to professional educators, but rather to include all of those individuals who have functioned as teachers for me. Some taught me how to teach just as others taught me how not to; some were intentional about their efforts just as others seemed quite oblivious to their involvement in such an enterprise. In short, anyone I have truly learned from has shaped my teaching self.

It is not uncommon to overhear a teacher claiming that he or she learns just as much from students as the students ostensibly learn from the teacher. While it is possible that for some this is little more than a stock expression which teachers are expected to present to others, I would contend that the teacher with the greatest potential to become a meaningful voice in the life of a student is one who truly believes it. This attitude encourages the teacher to include the perspective of the student in one's own understanding of self as teacher.

As I have sought to articulate the voices which have been meaningful to me as a teacher, the most consistent thread which connects them all can be simply described as personal interest. Reflecting upon those teachers who I feel have influenced me most brings me time and time again to people who were able to convey that the interest which drove their interaction with me was not just the fulfillment of a contractual obligation or a mere reflection of the interplay of our interconnected roles, but rather an interest in me as an individual. The difference here is between the teacher who asks a question of a student with the view that the answer is an efficient means to an end in the overall process of teaching and the teacher who asks a question of a student as a result of being truly interested in learning what that individual has to say. As a teacher, am I primarily interested in the product of a student's thought as a pedagogical device or as an expression of self which has meaning to me in and of itself? Of course, this is just another way of saying that it is important that the student feels that she or he "matters" to the teacher, not just as a student, but as the whole person who embodies that particular role.

I attribute much of my success as a student to those teachers who conveyed a personal interest in the classes they taught and who brought their lives into those classes. In turn, the successes that I have enjoyed as a teacher I can largely attribute to those situations wherein I was able to connect genuinely and personally with others so as to create a meaningful human conduit through which the form and content of subject matter could also be exchanged. All of this flows from the recognition that each class has a life of its own that I am responsible for jointly creating and maintaining with every individual who inhabits it. The personal validation of each and every member of the class therefore becomes a means of facilitating the educational process as well as an end in and of itself.

We ask our students to open themselves to new insights, experiences, and the views of others. This request carries with it the implicit expectation that the student will in essence become vulnerable to the impact of other selves, at the very least to the teacher's self. The student who feels that there is a fundamental level of personal concern evident for her or his individual self in the context of this expectation is more likely to feel empowered to take the risk(s) involved. The teacher who recognizes this should approach the classroom fully conscious of the need to establish his or her own vulnerability to the selves assembled therein.

The fact that this process is a reciprocal one can be illustrated through student reaction to a teacher's absence due to illness. Student reaction predicated on the centrality of the discharge of contractual obligation would revolve around the pragmatic implications of the absence itself, while student reaction predicated on the centrality of personal interest and connection would revolve around issues concerning the teacher's welfare. I would maintain that the teacher who is able to convey personal interest in the lives of her or his students would be more likely to engender mutual interest on behalf of said students and that this reciprocal personal interconnectedness would be reflected and reified as in the latter response described above. The issue here is one of whether we view ourselves (and are viewed by others) as submerged within and narrowly defined by the institutionalized status of teacher or as whole selves expressed through the role of teaching which is just one facet of who and what we are.

Viewing the self as a social production as opposed to an immutable core of being is critical to understanding the potential that we have to create a vital environment for learning together with our students. If individuals are capable of jointly creating, maintaining or even destroying selves through and within any given interaction itself, then teachers and students are engaged together in a process that goes far beyond the confluent dissemination and absorption of academic knowledge. Rather, teachers and students are engaging in the production of selves upon which the success or failure of the process ultimately hinges.

In pragmatic terms, this translates into creating and sustaining opportunities for intersubjective experiences in our relations with students. I feel that this must go beyond a superficial effort to "get to know our students" through contrived classroom rituals. Students must be encouraged to develop an awareness of their joint responsibility for making the class a world of their own, not just the teacher's world where students come to be serviced as they are passing through yet another tourist attraction on the way to some grand and final destination known as graduation. Of course, if students are perceived and treated as mere tourists by their "hosts," then we should expect them to eschew any notion of joint responsibility for the experience.

One general strategy for creating a sense of shared personal interest in the classroom is to involve students from the first day onward in the structuring of the life of the class. The fact that the student gains a sense of ownership with respect to the class operates as an enabling factor in construction of an efficacious sense of self for the student. In short, the student feels that her or his opinion really matters not only in terms of others caring about it, but also in that it can have a concrete impact on the reality at hand. Consequently, the student is receiving information that is self-validating from others and can integrate this information into the self that is being constructed and maintained both within the parameters of the class and beyond.

Any liberal arts college which claims to be committed to the process of educating the "whole person" must seriously examine what such a vision of education implies about the relationship between educators and students. Our efforts to realize such a mission will ultimately fall short if we embrace the notion that it can be accomplished merely by charging teachers with the task of exposing students to a variety of subjects and experiences that are purportedly designed to tap into the various components of the whole person (i.e., the physical, emotional, social, intellectual and spiritual aspects of self). While this is certainly an important aspect of the overall process, the content of that which is being taught must be understood as operating within the overall context of how it is being taught.

We must teach with the assumption that the intellectual self does not exist in a relational vacuum, but is instead an integral aspect of the whole self. The student brings the physical, the emotional, the social and the spiritual aspects of self into the classroom along with her or his intellectual self. So do we teachers. In this view, education becomes a "package" of sorts since we cannot truly help to develop any constituent part of the student self strictly in isolation from other aspects of the self. Educating the whole person is therefore accomplished largely through developing relationships between whole persons, not through the narrow development of various components of the self. Placing this discourse on the relationship between teaching and the self in the context of the education of K-12 teachers returns us once again to the significance of understanding what it means to say that one is a teacher.

If teachers accept the interpretation that what we do for a living is to disseminate knowledge to people narrowly defined as students, then we miss the opportunity to intentionally engage in what it is we are actually doing which is "building" people. Perhaps the analogy is crude and overly simplistic, but it effectively recognizes our involvement in the process of jointly constructing selves that we have been given unique access to by virtue of our position in their lives as teachers.

I can still vividly recall those experiences that I shared with teachers who somehow made my own voice seem worth listening to through their reactions to it. So many others had seemed to be saying that the only voice that really mattered in the social matrix at hand was their own. I opened my mind and my self to the former because I felt that their minds and selves were truly open to me while I offered only my brain (and provisionally, at that) to the latter because that is all they truly seemed concerned with.

It goes without saying that we need the voices of excellent teachers resounding throughout the entire educational spectrum, but the education of those who have chosen to become teachers themselves takes on a special meaning when one considers that much of how they will teach will be greatly influenced by how they were taught. For future K–12 teachers (and all future teachers) to view themselves as more than just disseminators of knowledge and agents of social control they must be taught by teachers who are willing to relate to them as whole persons who happen to be students. It is a rather simple equation: we must make a personal difference in the lives of our current education students if we expect them, as teachers, to make a real difference in the lives of their future students. This perspective, when translated through the teaching self, contains a message of fundamental significance for the student. Rather than saying: "I am interested in you learning because it is my professional obligation to help you accomplish learning," the voice that empowers our students to become teachers who will in turn empower others says: "I am interested in you; therefore I am interested in what we can accomplish through learning together."

Teaching of Quality

Joseph Buckley (Philosophy)
John Carroll University

In Robert Pirsig's *Zen and the Art of Motorcycle Maintenance* a pivotal event occurs when Sarah remarks to Phaedrus, "I hope you are teaching quality to your students."[1] Phaedrus tortures himself for days trying to pin down the elusive ghost of "Quality" while he claims to his students that they recognize it even though they may not be able to define it.

The quality of teaching is really the teaching of quality. Not fully understanding this insight is one of the reasons why we continue to argue and discuss about what constitutes the former. Everyone wants to "teach quality." Can anyone imagine college teachers admitting that they did not seek to do so? That they opted for mediocrity instead? It seems that we find ourselves in the same situation as Phaedrus' students. How can we recognize quality if we cannot define it? But we know what it is and we recognize it when we confront it. It is the sum total of what has happened in a course over a semester including the outcome if we have been successful in our teaching. Let me explain.

I take as my premise that teaching quality is the fundamental goal of instruction in a liberal arts college. The successful pursuit of this goal leads to effective teaching. The first class of every semester is a special experience; the academic world is new and fresh again. The students have not had the experience of this course before, and I have not had the experience of them either. The place where we meet is the place where they are—academically, intellectually, emotionally—not where I am. It is important to start where they actually are and not where some a priori template says that they *ought* to be.

Fine! Well, they're here! Where do we go now? My discipline is philosophy and I usually have a section or two of Introduction to Philosophy along with upper division courses in my specializations—logic and metaphysics. The discipline of philosophy dictates much of the scaffolding that structures our encounter. I find that the introductory course is the hardest one to teach; the quality of their first experience with philosophy usually determines how successful they are in subsequent courses. (At my college, every student takes three courses in philosophy as part of their core.) The approach I take to teaching is that philosophy is an activity; it is something that one *does* as opposed to something that one *suffers*. The difference is represented well by Gilbert Ryle's distinction between "knowing how" and "knowing that." Philosophy is an activity that one engages in and not a body of knowledge that one absorbs. So the process starts with the question of how to teach them to do philosophy, and, if successful, to do it with quality. How does it work?

As mentioned above, it is to start from the place where the students are. Well, where are they? If they are freshmen in an Introduction to Philosophy course, they are usually less than ninety days out of high school. High school has provided most of them with the educational experience that they will draw on in college. Add to this the fact that for most of them this is the first extended time away from home and family. When you put these two things together you realize that they are scared. They just do not know how they are going to measure up to the challenges and problems, academic and social, that they expect to encounter in college. If you also consider that many of them leave families which have serious problems, it is obvious that many freshmen are bringing some heavy baggage with them.

I do not want to give the impression that it is only the freshmen who are at this "place." Even with upperclassmen who have already taken one or more philosophy courses, there is apprehension upon starting a new course. There is often the anxiety of how they will measure up to a new set of problems and questions, a new professor, and new classmates. ("Was my

'A' in Intro a fluke?" "So I made the Dean's List! They were easy courses. What if she sees through me?") The problems may be mitigated but rarely dissolved. The upshot of all of this is that in many students self-confidence is lacking or only tenuously established in spite of a public persona of bravura.

Showing students how to do philosophy in such a context requires building their confidence and sense of self and at the same time developing the necessary conceptual skills. I find that this problem is exacerbated by the time factor; the acquisition of philosophical skills comes slowly. My experience is that in Introduction to Philosophy sections most of the students do not clearly demonstrate mastery of the techniques until around the eighth week of a fourteen week semester. In my attempts to keep them from becoming discouraged and psychologically "give up," I sometimes think I am the football coach of a team on a losing streak as well as the head cheerleader.

To keep them going until they reach the point in the course where they actually think that they can do it, you must begin by showing them that you care about them as the unique individuals that they are. This can be communicated in many ways. The first, and most obvious, is to learn their names; I can usually do this in three to four weeks. Then use the names wherever you run into them on campus. (I have known professors over the years who took the time to learn their students' names and then never used them!) After course change week I publish a student directory with their name, campus address, and telephone number. This looks like a minor point but I have found that it pays real dividends. I got the idea for the directory one semester when I was talking to a graduating senior. I mentioned a student (also a senior) who had been in class with him in his freshman year as well as several subsequent classes. I was surprised to find that he only knew her first name. The next day I asked each of my classes how many knew the last names of their classmates. There were only a handful in all the classes. A college populated by people with only first names!*

---

* Editor's note: Some colleges publish student directories arranged alphabetically BY FIRST NAMES in order to acknowledge the fact that students may not readily know each others' last names.

I also give them my home telephone number in the syllabus. They can call me any day of the week until 9 p.m. The upper limit is necessary for people who do not mean the same thing by "day" and "night" as the faculty. I have found that students who are reticent in class will often call me. This is a good opportunity to engage them in discussion and dialogue. It also helps to keep practical office hours and not those designed to minimize student consultation.

Never walk into any classroom without greeting whomever is there. I often say "Hello philosophers!" to them. This draws some puzzled looks, but it affords me an opportunity to tell them that if philosophers are those who do philosophy and they are doing philosophy, then they *are* philosophers. They even get used to hearing it by the end of the semester. All of these small things contribute to the building of trust and confidence in each other—our "social contract." The contract implies that the actions and behaviors of each of us have to be dependable if we are to create an environment in which learning can take place. Now I have taught long enough to know that the actions and behaviors of many 18 to 22 year olds are *not* always dependable. But this is rarely a problem since I have enough experience to anticipate or guess what will happen in most cases. It is mainly my actions and behaviors that I want them to feel at home with—no unpleasant surprises.

Even those elements of the course which are usually looked on as aversive and painful, such as tests, papers, and quizzes, can be interpreted in a positive light. My approach to tests (which are real workouts) is to get the students to view them as opportunities to show what they know, a chance to demonstrate their skills. I urge them to study together in small groups (having used their class directories to break the ice). This promotes a class solidarity and is also a confidence builder: since others are encountering similar problems, they realize they are not alone and know more than they think they did. The criticisms of the tests, papers, and quizzes are couched in terms of improvement. It is not that you are wrong (and branded with the letter "W") on this question but that this (answer, paper, etc.) could be improved by doing such and such. It is all directed at getting progress and improvement via what they have already achieved, not where they have failed.

Behind all of this, and as a saving virtue when the unex-
pected happens, my cardinal maxim is never take your self too
seriously. Philosophy is one of the most important and fun
things in my life but in no way is it going to be so for most of
my students. I feel no compulsion to "make them like it" as I
do; indeed such a task is impossible. I think that many teachers
suffer untold agony and depression because they take themselves too seriously and identify their disciplines with their
selves. When students do not respond positively, are indif-
ferent, or even hostile to some cherished concept, the teacher
often takes it as a personal rejection. With the frailties of our
common nature, it is probably impossible to totally eradicate
this tendency, but it must be resisted.

The setting most conducive to the teaching of quality resides
in the liberal arts college in my view. I do not think it an
exaggeration to claim that teaching remains its true core in
contrast to the multiversity with its plethora of often disparate
goals, each being guarded by its own constituency. The focus
of liberal arts teaching concerns the intellectual, emotional,
and moral lives of the students. Anything less than this is not
a true liberal arts college. A fundamental distinction, central
to carrying out this mission, must be made between training
and education. Training imparts the skills necessary to become
independent learners. Basic to this are the core skills of thinking, writing, reading, problem solving, and imagining. The
process of learning occurs when these skills are inculcated and
applied successfully. They enable students to become successful mathematicians, philosophers, linguists, etc.

Education is something qualitatively different. It is not the
end goal of education to prepare persons for defined careers.
Rather, education has as its continuing goal the preparation
of young women and men for a *life* as participants in a culture:
persons who are responsible, informed, aware, and self-conscious. One of the consequences of this distinction is that while
the skills of training are discipline-linked (originally in the
trivium and the quadrivium), education is not located in any
specific discipline or course but rather transcends all of them.
Education is not even limited to the exclusively academic
domain of the college, but is found in every nook and cranny
of college life and experience. Any attempt to confuse training

90

and education or to deny one of them can only lead to disaster and the failure of the liberal arts college. Certainly, you will still have an institution, one that can legally grant degrees but it is emphatically a liberal arts college, not, as Pirsig so aptly named it, a "church of reason."[2] How can this claim be supported?

If students are to take their place in a culture and perhaps make their own contribution to its growth and richness, they must be capable of leading meaningful and satisfying lives. But in order to create a meaningful life one has to have been able, at some point, to imagine that life or one very close to it. When students come to college at seventeen or eighteen, all that most of them have to go on is the way of life into which they have been socialized. This life may be good for them; it may be bad for them. But in any case it is usually not *theirs* as there has been no act of appropriation, of making it their own life. They are living almost exclusively by introjected values.

The crucial task facing women and men in college is to find (create?) a meaningful life with the help of all the possibilities offered by the liberal arts experience. This is accomplished by imagination more than by intellectual analysis. The question emerges: "Is this me?" The response: "Well, can you imagine it?"

One will not be able to find the meaningful life unless one can imagine oneself living it. If things go well they will succeed, though not without much trial and error (and tears). Each in its own way, the liberal arts disciplines stimulate the imagination to explore life's possibilities. The wondrous thing is that this does not depend exclusively on the subjects studied in any particular course or department. The most influential teachers I had in college were not necessarily those who taught me philosophy but ones who stimulated me to imagine the various elements comprising my notion of the ethical and cultural person.

So, one hopes, those who will some day venture into our elementary and secondary classrooms as well as into college teaching will learn not just what is said about a particular subject of study but what is shown—the broader vision of life, the insight into self. Then they can begin to comprehend and value the moral and cultural dimensions of their craft and bring this vision and insight to their own students. Through arts and sciences courses—the liberal arts—they gain knowledge of many academic disciplines, but also learn that the life of the teacher is far more than just knowing and teaching specific subject matter.

The teaching of quality is also necessarily connected with study, scholarship, and research. These three terms, however, do not adequately represent what is really at issue in quality teaching—the personal growth and maturation of the liberal arts teacher. This is a lifelong process and certainly a necessary condition for effective teaching. It seems trivial to remark how vital it is for college teachers to keep pace with the growing content of their subject fields, but this side of liberal arts teaching sometimes gets ignored. The exploration and mastery of the content is endless, but "content" is a bloodless word. What is involved here are problems, puzzles, and mysteries, the study of which is the true joy of the life of the mind. Behind them all stand the great *daimones* (life, death, grief, joy, sorrow, sex) that Euripides knew so well. To dilute proper content or freeze it into a time-warp with outdated notes and research is to kill the life spark of the teacher. Courses taught by such unfortunates involve little or no learning and become the academic version of the "valley of dry bones." Students intuitively sense when a teacher is merely going through the motions, rather than actively engaged in thinking out the problems anew and keeping up on current work and interpretations. Such a teacher is curious and excited by what is discovered and can communicate some of this to the class. Lacking this, students merely fulfill the course requirements by going through the motions; they have "psychologically" dropped out. This is a betrayal of them and of the ethos of the liberal arts college.

Of course there is another necessary condition omitted here: the responsibility that the college administration has to create the environment within which quality can be taught and studied. Without going into detail, two elements must be noted. College administrations have control over class load and class size. With rare exception, the number of classes a professor teaches and the number of students in those classes are definite and significant factor affecting the quality of the teaching and the learning that takes place. This must be bluntly asserted and *not* hedged with qualifications. It is embarrassing to have to mention these points; they ought to have been disposed of years ago. The sad fact is that they have not been relegated to the realm of old ignorances and are still too much with us. Students are usually paying a premium for the experience of the liberal arts college. One aspect of making this sacrifice worthwhile depends on restriction of course loads and class size so that the teaching of quality can happen. But as so many teachers sadly know, they are often the first to go whenever economic and political pressures accumulate.

In spite of all trials and troubles, I suspect that the liberal arts college, some form of which has been around since the twelfth century, will prevail and that quality *will* be taught through quality teaching.

Notes

1. Pirsig, R. M. (1979). *Zen and the art of motorcycle maintenance*. New York: William Morrow, 180.

2. Ibid., 148–53.

The Many Voices of the Classroom

Donna Marie Bauerly (English)
Loras College

I stood hesitantly at the classroom door to 9 Keane, a black moustache slightly tickling my upper lip, a snap-brim cap pulled down close to wire-rimmed glasses, my hands stuffed into the roomy pockets of an oversized trench coat. Instinctively, I reached to touch the soft leather of a billfold, where tucked away was a much-thumbed picture of the woman I had loved all of my adult life. The memory of her face gave me courage to walk into this group of 20th century college students and allow them to ask searching questions about my life and poems. Just stepping out of the 19th century, I felt a bit of the dislocation that moderns call "jet lag." But I could tell from the animation of the students in the brightly-lit room that they would be friendly to a gentle spirit. The students, grouped in small circles of four or five, were engaged in a lively exchange of ideas and questions. I listened for a moment more before entering the room.

Whose voice have you just heard? Was it truly that of the spirit of Edwin Arlington Robinson, sharing his thoughts just before he joined the literature class studying modern American poetry? Or, was it my voice, that of a persona, qualitatively distanced from that of Robinson—distanced by time, by mortality, by gender?

Voice. For me, a multiplicity of voices has always been a hallmark of excellent teaching. Before I tune in to what I consider a "chorus of the classroom," however, let me sketch

94

first for you—as one example of voice—what happened in order for "Edwin Arlington Robinson" to stand outside the classroom door of 9 Keane.

Introductory first-day "lectures" can be very boring, particularly if students do not seem ready yet for the class at hand. Always searching for better ways to present that opening, to find a way of maximum involvement right from the start, I chose the summer of 1990 as a perfect time for interactive classroom drama. Some of the students in this class were already used to my unorthodox methods, and I counted on them to bring the rest along. Summer teaching of three-hour stretches gave time to accomplish the preparation necessary for this "drama," and I needed an interim period for my own preparation since I wanted nothing else but to join the class in the midst of its first discussion on Robinson—as Edwin Arlington Robinson himself.

First, I read and re-read as much of Robinson's poetry as I had time for, especially the poems I included on the syllabus. Then I read two or three biographies of Robinson, plus a number of recent critical articles about him, his times and his poetry. I **became** Robinson, reading his poems and his life from inside out! Eventually, I placed a few good portraits of Robinson on the bulletin board in 9 Keane among the faces of the many other modern and contemporary poets we would consider. I would call attention to one particular portrait of Robinson, with wire-rim glasses and a black moustache, dressed in a trench coat and a snap-brim cap!

On the opening day of class, after a brief introduction to modern poetry, I assigned the students to groups of four or five, parceling out a Robinson poem to be read aloud by each one: "Richard Cory," "Luke Havergal," "Mr. Flood's Party," "The Mill," and "Miniver Cheevy." These poems have at least one outstanding central character. "The Mill" has two: a miller and his wife. All of the poems are readily accessible in a first reading and lull the students into thinking that reading poetry is lots easier than they ever thought it was (a desirable side-effect). I had a chronology of Robinson's life duplicated for them so they could raise questions of biographical interest, if they so chose. After all poems had been heard, students were to **become** the central character of the poem they read and be able to answer questions from the other "characters" in their own group about thoughts, motivations, desires and so forth. As a role-model, I first read "Bewick Finzer," another Robinson poem, became Bewick for a short time, and anticipated some questions I could answer, if asked.

Each student printed the name of her "persona" on a piece of paper and stood it up on the desk as a name tag. After ten minutes of silent preparation, to look over their assigned poems, to search for insights into their personae, and to think of questions to ask one another, the "drama" began.

Such polyphony (four groups of students reading at the same time, each group intent on the one student reading in their particular circle) is often freeing for students who are shy about sharing with others. I usually leave the classroom briefly, when students begin to read or discuss, giving them even more freedom for interpretation and leadership.

When the Robinson poems had been read and the questions had begun, I returned, sat at my desk, and listened. I saw students pointing to the pictures on the board, referring to the chronology of Robinson at times, or rechecking lines from poems, interacting with one another as Robinson's characters reborn. After twenty minutes or so, I quietly left the room again, picked up my new clothes from the teachers' lounge, changed into Edwin Arlington Robinson in the women's restroom nearby, attaching the moustache firmly with doubled-sided tape. I had cut the black hair off my poodle's long earlocks that very morning! When I looked at myself in the mirror, I saw a real transformation. I felt convincing, even to the men's shoes I wore.

This time, when I entered the classroom, a couple of students looked up, looked away—then, gasped and looked again. When all were staring my way, I introduced myself and said that their teacher had told me they sometimes sat in one large circle and held a general discussion. I asked if they would like to do that now and find out from me, Edwin, about my life and poems.

Some of the students retained their own "personae" as Robinson's characters and quizzed me about my motivations in creating them. Some students became themselves again and raised other questions. Some chuckled and went along with it all; some took it very seriously. When it was all over, I wondered if I had learned more than they had. What I knew for sure was the value of role-playing. I understood Edwin Arlington Robinson as never before and realized why so many of my students love the various role-playing exercises I do frequently in all my classes, even my freshman composition courses.

Role-playing is perhaps the best way to experiment with "voice," and I have learned to structure the situations so that the entire class benefits. Usually I assign the roles far in advance so the students can prepare thoroughly. Sometimes I ask them to become characters in a drama or short story such as in "The Short Happy Life of Francis Macomber," where Francis, Margot, and Wilson form an intriguing trio to question. The performances can be startling sometimes, especially if the students take the situation seriously, dress the part, and become very convincing in their portrayals. All students are expected—before the class itself—to write down questions for each character, zeroing in on "why" and "how" questions, staying close to the text or branching out into milieu and motivation for an author if an author is part of the questioning. Characters may quiz each other if they so choose, and students may ask "follow up" questions that prolong a certain line of questioning. Performers sit at the front of the classroom, usually in a kind of semi-circle. A student leader, sitting at the teacher's desk, calls on students who have questions to ask. I sit at the back or side of the room, tally the questions asked by each student and assign a grade for student participation as well as for the students who actually perform.

Some very tense situations have developed. Linda, from Miller's *Death of a Salesman,* protected her husband Willy so successfully that the student who asked about the rubber hose and Willy's suicide thoughts, was silenced thoroughly by Linda's icy reply, "What rubber hose?" Popeye, from Faulkner's *Sanctuary,* managed to intimidate not only Temple Drake, but the entire class! Character interactions from Frost's "Death of a Hired Man" and "Home Burial" have stunned student questioners into an awed respect for grief.

Student voices are extended and freed in these role-playing exercises. They learn to think and react as someone else would think and react—even someone of a different time or gender or race.

Small group discussions always provide ways to extend student voices. These discussions need to be planned carefully and monitored so they don't degenerate into gossip sessions. But most students address themselves willingly to such participation, particularly if they feel other students in their groups come prepared for an intelligent interchange. In the American Renaissance class that I teach, I use an exercise from psychology for group dynamics about a young man and woman who lived on two separate islands divided by shark-infested waters. The way these two get together and the aftermath make for an interesting fight (and fight, it is) over value systems. In the midst of the furor, I stop their small-group discussions and turn to the story for the day, "Rappaccini's Daughter," and I ask them to order the characters in this short story of Hawthorne's according to moral integrity: 1=most moral; 4=least moral. The characters, if you remember, are: Rappaccini, Beatrice (his daughter), Baglioni, and Giovanni. That fight is as heated as the two-island story, since the directive is to come up with one common list. Of course, I never expect that to happen, and it doesn't! But no one ever assumes again that there are easy answers for Hawthorne's complexities.

Students keep a critical journal in literature as well as composition classes. I ask for their initial reactions to stories or essays—reactions from the voice of the heart as well as the head. I collect excerpts from these journals, pages from a looseleaf notebook, excerpts chosen by the students themselves. In parts of this Journal I ask for a more informed "voice" to speak, the voice of the student who has read the story, poem or essay more than once, talked about it with friends, perhaps even gone to the library to read about it. Sometimes I am even more directive, assigning certain questions concerning character, plot, setting, symbol, irony, point of view. This voice responding is the "student critic" voice, more formal yet still personal.

I have also assigned "browsing cards" lately—4 by 6 index cards on which they tell me about some library browsing they have done and what "connections" they have made to any class they're taking and to the lives they live. When they ask me "What do you want us to find?" (a typical question which saddens me some), I ask them if they ever go to the Mall to just browse. "Of course." And what do you look for? "Oh, anything, nothing." Well, that's what I want you to do in the library—just go look, open your eyes and mind wide and just look. Follow your instincts. Do you sometimes find something good when you just browse while you're shopping? "Oh, yes! I found. . . ." And usually the eyes light up with remembrance. That's what I'm looking for in the "browsing cards." These voices are some of the most interesting I hear. I don't always expect students to share these "BC's" but I give them the opportunity to do so, re-collecting them from those willing to "publish" them on the classroom wall. Students from many classes "hear" these voices and often comment.

Many of the students I teach want to become teachers; many of them are in teacher-training courses. My classroom is one of their places for teacher-training. The voices we share now will eventually echo out in many other classrooms when they have assumed the teacher-role. Students often teach as they are taught. I know I do. As a child I went to a laboratory school, taught by some of the best teachers from an excellent order of teaching nuns. I watched young teachers trained by these outstanding women, and without knowing it, I absorbed all kinds of excellent teaching methods. I knew, for sure, that teaching was an active event, that learning was just as active. When I think of grade school, I remember motion. We were always doing something: putting on a play; writing music or stories, or poems; going to the fire station; becoming the life cycle of the monarch butterfly; giving "assemblies" for parents, for other classrooms, even for ourselves. Learning was exciting, kaleidoscopic. So I teach, as I was taught. Hopefully, so will some of my students.

I choose two student assistants, usually junior or senior writing majors, for my composition sections. Their voices enrich my own. They attend the Monday discussion and theory classes, and when we "workshop" student papers each Wednesday, these student assistants take over half the class. We divide the classroom into two groups of ten. The papers are handed in the Monday before with copies for their own groups. Five papers can be workshopped one week; five the next. All sorts of preparation is behind this workshopping: preparation between the student helpers and me; preparation in the classroom for good pre-writing and workshop sessions. Often, individual evaluation guides are necessary for in-depth and meaningful reaction from student critics. The sessions themselves improve with age, but take loads of energy and good organizing so that the interaction of students with students (one-on-one or one with a group) doesn't degenerate into a passive acceptance of any kind of writing. But, I have found that the dedication of the student assistants who often want to make their way in the world by their writing are a kind of inspiration to these young freshmen fledgling writers that I, with all my own writing dedication, cannot be. Sometimes these student assistants also work (through Work Study) in our Writing Center as well and become quite professional in interactions with their peers.

Interaction with other professors is yet another way of extending voice. Over the years I have team-taught such interdisciplinary courses as: Rhetoric (teaming with composition, speech and logic teachers), American Drama and Alienation (teaming with a philosophy professor), and Literature and Film (teaming with a drama professor). All-College Honors courses that I have conceived, planned, and coordinated have been the most challenging: Nothing (taught by nine professors with topics that varied from "Black Holes" to the music of John Cage to the short story "Bartleby the Scrivener" to the "Empty Set" in mathematics), The Doppleganger (taught by eleven professors with multiple doubles everywhere), and Creativity and Depression (taught by thirteen professors) in which we examined the possibility and the probability of a link between the two, from the perspective of many disciplines.

Team-teaching allows for a multi-perspective and a chorus of voices from the various disciplines brought to bear on some important theme or issue. These are questioning courses, often most uncomfortable both for teachers and students alike. We are never quite sure of where we are heading. We just set sail, certain of the fact that we have an excellent crew and can weather most storms. After all, it's the "horse latitudes" of the teaching world that are the most distressing. When we are compelled to question one another, when the real questions are asked, when we are secure enough in our ability to seek even when we don't always find, this is most freeing for our students who often want to question but feel too insecure to do so.

Next fall semester, I will teach my composition course differently, conjuring up an even wider variety of voices. A new approach to composition is really nothing new, however, for I am always most dissatisfied with this course; and I have taught it differently many times. "Voice" may be an important factor in making that tough-teaching course more palatable to all of us. What will be qualitatively different in this new way is that I have invited eight professors from a variety of disciplines to choose an essay from their field that: (1) is accessible to most freshmen; (2) is challenging and interesting to those freshmen; (3) is an excellent example of writing in that particular discipline, in content, form, and methodology; and (4) is provocative of some reaction from those who read the essay. The professors will introduce these essays at different times during the semester, telling why they chose them, and why they chose their own discipline for advanced study—even why they chose teaching as a profession. They will also recommend certain library resources for in-depth study in that discipline. This input from excellent teachers in various disciplines may take only fifteen or twenty minutes on a specified Monday morning, but I am hoping that the combined chorus of so many excellent voices coming from a wide spectrum of academic pursuits will assist students in their liberal arts education voyage.

On Fridays, I enlist the "voices" of our college librarians since I go with my freshman composition classes every week to the library to pursue research. During the first semester we learn sources in an organized fashion; this coming fall I will add the dimension of following the academic disciplines as we take them up in the classroom. During the second semester, students develop an independent argumentative research paper, using all the methodology knowledge they have amassed the first semester. Their own personal voices become strengthened by in-depth listening to a multitude of voices, some who agree with a chosen point of view, some who violently disagree. These Friday library sessions give me and the student assistant time to hear the individual student voice, in the process of search. Conferences with students are easier and more meaningful when there is this on-going and predictable interaction with them.

We have begun a mentoring program at our college. At first, the relationship was between students and professors. Recently, we have branched out to add a new dimension, mentoring by our seasoned teachers for our youngest and newest colleagues. I will be able to do nothing better for a new professor than to invite that person to join in on the chorus of voices I already hear in my classroom. When I began teaching, at age nineteen, it was in a junior high school, and I was observed frequently and given on-going encouragement and constructive criticism. On days when our school was not in session and other schools in the area were, we often visited the classrooms of other teachers and learned by watching or participating.

College teachers, even as teaching assistants, if they were so lucky, might not have had much constructive criticism, perhaps not even much of a role model. Those of us who are fortunate enough to be considered excellent teachers, recognized as such by our own students, peers and administrators, have an obligation, it seems to me, to pass on at least something of the "how" and the "why" of that recognition. Some of what constitutes excellent teaching can be taught.

As one of the freshman registration counselors (one-on-one advisement and scheduling of first and second semester classes), I contact during the summer before their first year about 80 entering students. In order to continue responsible advisement of these students, I have "extended my own advisement voice" by inviting six other professors to join me in this academic counseling. Working together, sharing our ideas and concerns, we can create another kind of chorus, one that is most harmonious for our students. When they see a concerted effort toward their good, they may be more inclined to enter into that process for themselves.

Many voices in our college environment can enrich our own in what can be a classroom of "song": whether solo or group, whether harmony or cacophony, whether silence. What power, what joy, we can free through this camaraderie of voice.

102

Other People, Other Stories, *Ours*

Harvey L. Klevar (Anthropology)
Luther College

Attempts to capture beginnings, to translate experiences—cosmic, social, or personal—are always interwoven into the tapestry of stories. Looking backward, story-tellers incorporate signs, events, figures and values into those tales and myths they believe will help explain life as it is variously lived. So it is that the Genesis account and Darwin's story of human origins, *The Aeneid* and America's Westerns, family histories, and personal biographies all are documents studied by those seeking understandings of how what is came to be.

I also explore stories—my personal, the human, and our national ones—to try to explain how it was that I teach teachers-to-be as I do.

Born on a small, Texas coastal farm to Czech parents with strong ties to an extended ethnic family, I did not speak much English until I began school. There I initially smarted with shame when I was placed into the lowest level "black-bird" reading group. I subsequently altered my language, behavior, and interests to meet expectations of teachers, peers and community. My classmates attended different churches and carried "store-bought bread" sandwiches for lunch, but otherwise I perceived myself as almost indistinguishable from other local children.

How different I remained in their estimations I did not realize until my high school years. Then, kiddingly I thought, the fellows began calling me a "dumb bohunk." Those instances I uneasily laughed aside. My academic and athletic achievements argued otherwise, I told myself. One day, however, a youth, recently transferred to our school from the piney woods area of Texas, heard the bohunk reference. He stood with slack-mouthed amazement: his daddy always had told him that "bohunks wuz black like niggers." And not until years later did I discover why it was that young ladies seldom would date me more than twice. By then mature, one confessed, "Our parents were afraid we'd become serious about you. They didn't want us marrying a Czech and a Catholic."

Upon graduation I felt I had to convince myself and others that I wasn't dumb. I became the fifth person in the forty year history of the school to attend college. Summer work in a Minnesota boys' camp broadened my parochial horizons. In the Midwest there seemed to be no prejudice against Czech ethnics. I relocated there and eventually began teaching high school English in a small, central Minnesota town.

During my seven years there I learned much. Wordsworth, agreements between subjects and verbs, and *Macbeth* did not interest the students; they were more interested in challenging the teacher. Trying to pull them to my elevated literary level strained us all. Desperation led me to discover a teaching basic: Learning must begin at the level of the students' experiences, including stories about illegal forays into bars, poems about hunting epiphanies, and the drama of domestic conflicts. Writing such accounts then made grammar a concern for them. Their attempts to translate experience into words made them also more companionably sympathetic even to Wordsworth and Shakespeare.

Other things I learned were not so satisfying. Shortly after I arrived in the community, I discovered that the Midwest practiced exclusions as cruel as those of my childhood region. Here the people of color were the Indians, the Chippewa, the Anishinabe victims. This was most evident in the schools, where their histories, their values, and even their presences were discounted. Well intentioned though I was, I attempted to teach them with a mournfully insensitive ignorance. I gradually recognized there was much I did not know.

104

My interests in American literature and culture pointed me towards seeking a masters degree in American Studies. That introductory experience opened so many doors to understanding—one marked anthropology—that I remained to earn my Ph.D. That degree argued, moreover, that I was not a "dumb" bohunk.

Hired by Luther College, I was partially assigned to teach English methods and supervise student teachers and otherwise to teach English and American literature. Challenging and satisfying though those assignments proved to be, seven years later I received an intriguing invitation. The Anthropology director wished me to do some retraining and to join the Program to teach cultural anthropology full time. I had two days to decide.

That hurried choice was one of the most fortunate of my life. The varieties of my subsequent cultural awakenings are too staggering to chart. Yet one still-evolving hypothesis is so compelling that its application has altered forever my interpretation of the human story. That version revises intrinsic theories about humans and their relationships with the cosmos, the earth, and each other. And because it so essentially informs my life and teaching—and a course required of all Luther's prospective teachers—its basics invite telling.

The traditional secular story is one sacredly familiar to most people of European heritage. Our uncivilized, animal-like ancestors competed for scarce resources by law of claw and club. Eventual domestication of plants and animals promoted a progress towards security and communities where a division of labor created ever more sophisticated art and architecture. Reason applied to nature produced an abundance of resources unimagined by our primitive ancestors. Through a chain of being, with humans just below the angels, God gave them "dominion over the birds of the air and the beasts of the field." That father-like being demanded that they transform the unproductive, undeveloped wilderness into an abundant garden. Those who so sacredly labored would deservedly reap the rewards: a cornucopia of food, a wealth of labor-saving inventions, tools and machines, a harnessing of famine and disease.

Reason—science—applied to all aspects of the cosmos, nature and human behavior eventually would lead to a paradise regained. Patriarchs, priests, and kings: to them was given dominion over the earth and its "undeveloped regions," over its creatures and rivers, over its unenlightened or unchosen people, over women, children, and the defeated. Every story, every teaching emphasized that truth.

Their stories became our sacred and secular texts. Jacob and Laban bartering daughters and concubines for flocks, Odysseus slaying Penelope's suitors, and nation-founding Aeneas sacrificing Dido for empire: such stories we teach as lessons. Other figures, other stories: Alexander the Great, Hannibal, and Sir Lancelot; and in our nation: Kit Carson, General Schwarzkopf and John Wayne, Benjamin Franklin, Andrew Carnegie and J.P. Morgan, Henry Ford, Lee Iacocca and Sam Walton. All are familiar because their examples are used variously to teach the values of conquest, accumulation, and competition.

Other figures and events we celebrate for their contributions to subduing the forces of cosmos and space. Archimedes and Galileo, James Watt and the Wright Brothers, the Panama Canal and the transcontinental railroad: what they have stood for has taken us from harnessing horses to harnessing the atom, from conquering crab grass to conquering space. These stories we teach to our student generations because they energize those myths, values, and practices we have enshrined as sacred truths.

All resonate with two common themes: that the natural condition of human life is one of a constant struggle to balance between extremes and that a rational order is the ultimate good. Thus all conflicts between mind and body, "man" and nature, the state and the individual, the rich and the poor must be resolved through reason and force. Wilderness, oceans, and space are to be conquered. Flooding rivers and students must be controlled. Emotions and passions must be leashed. (I ask my students: how many ecstatic bursts of reason can you recall?) That imperative is so pervasive that it even determines our perceptions of beauty. Most things bright and beautiful are those which are domesticated and controlled: geometrically platted fields and towns, carefully sculpted flowers, shrubs and lawns, finely orchestrated pieces of music, art or writing. We see through the eyes of the culture which defines us.

Too easily we forget that for countless millennia humans did not so order and perceive their world. I, therefore, tell that earlier story, one recreated through hints and guesses from a variety of sources. Some are strained from the experiences of a broad range of preliterate peoples: the First Americans, the First Australians, the First Africans. Others are borrowed from the studies of feminine revisionists such as Ruth Bleiers's *Science and Gender* and Sarah Blaffer Hardy's *The Woman that Never Evolved,* from Elizabeth Fisher's *Women's Creation* and Riane Eisler's *The Chalice and the Blade* and from Richard B. Lee's "The Hunters: Scarce Resources in the Kalahari." Bits and pieces assimilated from elsewhere I have assumed as my own perhaps subconsciously.

That story: once upon a time, long long ago, bands of humans evolved to roam the earth, foraging and scavenging. Gradually they became creatures of wonder who etched cave drawings and buried their dead. Eventually they reasoned that survival called for living harmoniously with nature and, to a somewhat lesser degree, with each other. They carefully studied nature—the heavens, the plants, and creatures of the earth—because their living depended upon that knowledge. Seasons and migrations and fruitings directed their wanderings, their dwellings, and all within their cultures and beliefs. A beneficent being had given the earth and all of its creatures to their trust. Because all beings, from stars and rocks to birds and humans, had been woven equally into an intricate and sacred web, they had to revere it all equally, had to maintain it unspoiled from generation to generation. To violate it, to change it in any way would question the wisdom of the femininized source of all life, would diminish the beauty of a sacredly charged universe. Some violations were essential; all beings had to harvest and kill to eat. Yet the balance could be restored through rituals of acknowledgement and thanks, through singing the world back into harmony. (Something like reseeding strip-mined areas?) In that Edenic garden all worked to survive, but they did not labor to dominate and control nature.

Then for reasons unknown—population pressures? a sense of security during scarce seasons?—some 12,000 years ago (only a blink in the continuum of human kind) someone, some peoples began domesticating plants and animals. No longer were they bending to nature's leads; they were manipulating nature to meet their needs. Then no longer did they study cosmic orbits and plant and animal habits to harmonize symbiotically with them. They studied them instead for the knowledge to alter their habits and habitats, to increase a production their labor claimed as their own. Nature no longer could be accepted as the freely sacred repository of all life, the beneficent provider. It instead was reinterpreted as a plot to be cultivated, a range-herd to be managed, a territory to be defended or expanded through force of arms. Labor and tools, weapons and control had given them that right to power. With production and increase as the measure, the ancestors of Jacob and Laban had to desensitize themselves to the feminized and productive forces of life, to the earth with its plants and animals, to women as both producers of children and laborers.

Because such patriarchs gradually assumed control and proprietary rights over all production and its increase, the respect previously reserved for nature was transferred to them. Survival itself demanded that allegiance. Not mother nature but an arbitrary father-provider would now control and dictate, redistribute or deny, all necessary resources to those he chose. That right devolved from God the Father who had declared an end to the hunting and gathering Eden, who demanded instead that Eve, the life-force, be subject to the masculine Adam and that they and their descendants thereafter should survive through sweat-of-the-brow labor.

Transfer of power to the patriarchs of reward and punishment likewise granted them the vantage of story. Without question or sanction Laban could barter Leah and Rachel to Jacob. Agememnon could sacrifice Iphigenia to free his war fleet to sail. Henry VIII could behead wives and lieges. Kings had power over serfs and popes, over their flocks. Servants were to be obedient to masters whether in Israel or on a Southern plantation. Laborers were to be unquestioningly grateful to vineyard owners, General Motors, and the Iowa Beef Processors. Wives were to be subject to their husbands, and children to their parents and teachers. Those who claimed the property and resources, who controlled the knowledge and tools had indisputable rights over the dispossessed. Power and control, reward and punishment rightfully trickle down through a sacred hierarchical social order our stories teach us.

Only after I had sought and mused anthropologically for a long while did I realize how hierarchical myth determines practically every aspect of human life in our post-hunting-gathering world. Almost all human energies—national, institutional, and personal—are devoted to maintaining control and dominance, to structuring a social order based upon power, privilege, and force.

On the most elemental level of physical survival, the control, manipulation and adapted use of nature consumes an inordinate amount of human effort. Forests are leveled, land is tilled, and herbicides are sprayed; cars are manufactured, purchased, and maintained; oil wells are drilled and highways are paved; rivers are dammed or diverted; and atoms are split and contained. More energy and money are devoted to controlling dandelions and lawns than are spent nationally on education. All of this so that we might shape nature's forces to our desires rather than readapt to its unrestrained bounty.

The human costs of social dominance and control are no less taxing. All government at every hierarchical level, through all of its institutions, has as its charge the control of its citizens, and sometimes those of other nations as well. Policies, guidelines and laws, military forces and police, prisons and wars are all institutionalized in the name of social control and selective justice. Hierarchically defined churches, courts, and schools use punishments and rewards to achieve similar ends.

As if such various determinations were not conscriptive enough, that model for "rationalizing" human behavior shapes even families and individuals within a social order. Almost all work is either directly or indirectly performed to keep nature at bay. Money is earned for house payments and car payments, for gas and electric bills, for health care and labor saving tools of various types. On the social level husbands and wives often joust and battle for control; witness the instances of spouse abuse. Conflicts between parents and children spin around issues of rule. On the individual level people jog and diet to master their bodies, and so we variously subjugate and adapt those forces of nature which otherwise would define us so differently.

Such interpretations of humans in their environments shape almost all of my anthropological tellings of the human story. Most pervasively, however, they inform an American Minorities course required of all education majors as part of their human relations component. Because of my own Texas experiences as a minority within a dominant regional culture, I resonate more sympathetically to this offering than to some of the others which I teach. In both content and method, therefore, I have integrated personal experiences, understandings, and philosophy to structure the course.

Most Luther College students have accepted uncritically the legitimacy of the stories told by the dominant society for making judgments about American minorities. Consequently, during the first three weeks of the course I refocus and challenge those values and institutions which exact their demands from all who live in America. The larger development model (i.e., improving upon nature through reason, technology and labor), the sacred Anglo-Saxon imperatives of private property, language and law, and the Puritan celebrations of work and wealth as signs of salvation: these are identified as the constants informing all institutions—legal, social and religious—and judgments of ourselves and others. Appropriate readings—from *Conquest of Paradise, Living Poorly in America, Prosperity Lost,* and *Dignity*—and films such as *Los Sures* and *Poletown Lives* are keyed with my revisionist's version of the American myth which defines us all.

Once the domains of that dominant story have been mapped and challenged as socio-cultural constants, the course summarily explores the experiences of America's other people and the stories they live and tell. First Americans and African Americans, Latinos and women, Southeast Asians, and the sexually different define the specific units. Allusions to the handicapped, elderly, and children serve as reminders that they also are exceptions to the homogenous norm.

For each respective group the format is the same. Through summary lectures (the classes are distressingly large) or more accurately, through cultural stories, the experiential histories and values of the people are sketched. Coincident to such generalizations are outside readings—studies, accounts, and stories—which specifically elaborate upon the socio-historical briefs. Because the classes are too unwieldy for visits to distant reservations or urban enclaves, to ghettos or barrios, I use films and resource people from the respective groups to fill the gap between abstractions and the living experience. The more culturally inclusive visual story balanced by personalized minority testimony helps students empathize with people whose stories previously have been told by those outside the respective experience.

In addition to regular class attendance and faithful completion of collateral readings, students are expected to write association papers complementing each unit. They link an issue identified in class or readings with something they have read or seen, heard or experienced outside the class context. Thus I seek to encourage application of classroom learning to daily living.

Though the American Minorities course is traditional in some respects, it is perhaps most unorthodox in the areas of student evaluation and grading. Because both have stressed individualized, competitive ranking methods—grades being used primarily to categorize individuals for society's institutional convenience—I attempt to counter that emphasis in favor of learning. Long before the exercise is due, I distribute a range of topics which demand integration of theory with the specifics of the respective group experiences. Individuals or self-combined groups of students are to choose one topic, prepare it beforehand and then write it within an hour's limit for submission by the scheduled date. Almost without fail I return the "integration exercises" with comments and grades on the subsequent class day. The grades, however, are not carved in stone; if dissatisfied, individuals or groups may revise until they have earned the grade they desire. Such latitude is especially appropriate for those who initially misunderstood the expectations or for international students who perhaps were reluctant to seek clarifications of confusions.

What ultimate effects my different versions of the human and American stories, my approaches to evaluation and grading have upon prospective teachers, I do not know. I trust that most gain fresh perspectives and sensitivities which eventually will make them more empathetically inclusive in their teaching at whatever level and that they will test with more emphasis upon learning than ranking. My hope is that because we are all myopically biased by the stories our dominant culture teaches us, they actively will seek other stories to tell and teach. Those especially which are told through our nation's minority voices demand sharing.

Dominant America long has compelled others variously to learn, and conform to, its myths. For just as long we have discounted and ignored those other American stories—from First Americans and African Americans, from women and people of different orientations. The time has come to listen and learn. Their experiences and values offer understandings and wise considerations for us all: other people, other stories, ours.

Good Role Models are Hard to Find: Chasing the Mystery

Jesse L. Scott (History)
Newberry College

W ho cares about the past?" "Wherein lies the value of history?" "Why should anyone bother learning about things that happened far away and long ago?" In short, "Why study history?"

These are a few of the questions students have voiced time and again over the years. When asked by people sitting in our classrooms, they have perplexed, sometimes even frightened, trained historians and professional educators teaching other disciplines who recognize the essential value of knowledge of the past and who are certain of its usefulness. Maybe Professor Stephen D. Brookfield is right. "Teaching," he wrote, "is the educational equivalent of white-water rafting . . . All teachers sooner or later capsize, and all teachers worth their salt regularly ask themselves whether or not they are doing the right thing."[1] I certainly know the sensation. Some days I feel all wet! However painful, these are fair questions our students ask of us, and they deserve responses.

After all, good teachers, we are told, can teach anything— even history! But what is good teaching? When I am confronted by confounding circumstances in the classroom or the hallowed halls of academe, frequently that question comes to mind. That question seems ever present. It is a gnawing one: What is good teaching? And likewise, whenever that question begins to prey on my mind I always remember an episode from my own days as a student. In remembering I find the courage to dry myself off, crawl back into the classroom, and at least try to answer those tough questions. Please allow me to explain.

Years ago in 1979 Professor Donald M. McKale stood before us in a well-used classroom in Hardin Hall at Clemson University in South Carolina. On that day he delivered his final presentation of that semester. As he had time and time before, Professor McKale began to speak with authority but also calmly with enthusiasm and sincerity. He masterfully unfolded to us yet another organized, carefully written episode. As always he was giving a telling and lucid story of humanity's past and hinting at its importance to us and to generations to come. We listened closely. We were eager to know what we might learn from him that day as we so often did throughout the semester. Once again Professor McKale challenged us to think, encouraged us to understand our motivations and those of others, urged us to respect other people, to carry a sense of justice with us in all matters, and to have above all courage and faith in ourselves. The world would one day be ours, and it would be our responsibility to make history an even more magnificent story for generations to come. Professor McKale unraveled for us the value of studying history: History was taking place all around us all the time.

All too quickly the hour passed. Professor McKale concluded. Silence momentarily dominated the room and all in it. First one student, then another, then three or four others, and suddenly all thirty or so students began to applaud, and we continued until the room was filled with smiling faces all determined to give something in return to this person who had so skillfully and carefully won our confidence and appreciation. And Professor McKale . . . well, he stood before us, hands in pockets, smiling—maybe even blushing—and seeming to embrace us all. Words were no longer necessary. We were sure we had convinced him that we were indeed worthy of his care, his efforts, and his knowledge. Never before had I witnessed, and have yet again to see, students make such heroic efforts to show a faculty member that they truly appreciated one's willingness to give and to give and to give.

For those of us who were there that semester it was crucial that he knew how much we appreciated what he had given us. Professor McKale had given us heart, and we knew it. Even to this day, I still take heart whenever I remember that moment. For me that single episode in 1979 captures a glimpse of the level of accomplishment that an educator may reach in teaching today's youth.

Thinking about Professor McKale urges me to consider the words of another person whom I greatly admire. Several years ago while he was visiting our Newberry College campus in South Carolina Professor Parker Palmer made a lasting impression on me. I will always remember him. He once wrote, "Only when we take heart as professors can we 'give heart' to our students—and that, finally, is what good teaching is all about."[2] But how did Professor McKale ever manage it? About that I am not sure. It's all a mystery to me.

What I am certain about is that the subuniverse of education needs more people like Professor McKale. We need more people who are not afraid of what Professor Parker Palmer describes as a "matter of living the mystery." No doubt Professor McKale ranks as an educator of educators. Role models are fundamental. What I remember is that with ease and skill he always delivered his cogently written and telling presentations in a lively manner that stimulated and involved even the least interested minds. He told a good story with admirable understanding. His control and insight allowed him to tell stories of the past—tragedies and glories as well as hate and love—that became vividly imaginable and understandable to us all. As Professor Palmer has explained, "good teachers help students see the persons behind the ideas, persons whose ideas often arose in response to some great suffering or hope that is with us still today."[3]

Regardless of the subject matter, Professor McKale lectured with vigor, a sense of scholarly fairness, and a rationally guided feeling that challenged the brightest students to think, to seek more information and that enabled even the least accomplished ones to understand. Nobody was excluded from Professor McKale's semester journey through the past. He encouraged us all to participate in discussions, to question his evidence and conclusions, to challenge his ideas, and most of all he asked of us all that we learn to listen closely and to think.

"Good teaching, whatever its form," wrote Professor Palmer, "will help more and more people learn to speak and listen in the community of truth, to understand that truth is not in the conclusions so much as in the process of conversation itself, that if you want to be 'in truth' you must be in the conversation."[4]

With Professor McKale we were a part of the process. He included us in the "community of knowing.[5] Also I remember that Professor McKale's expectations and academic standards were rigorous. Goals established for his students were high, but able to be reached. When appropriate he was stern, but he was equally kind and concerned. Above all, Professor McKale was good-natured and optimistic; he motivated all of his students, though in varying degrees, to achieve and to strengthen their capabilities.

His relentless patience and his willingness to guide encouraged and enabled us to complete required readings, to tackle exams with hope, and to write papers with a determination to improve with each effort. While he guided the average student through the material, he encouraged the brighter ones to go beyond course requirements and to learn to teach themselves. Now that was good teaching! (Once while attending a conference, I heard a colleague remark that she attempts to teach in ways that will enable and encourage her students to learn more about a subject than she knows. That goal is consistent with Professor McKale's.)

But still, the question remains? What is good teaching? Or, what is effective teaching? "Good teaching," wrote Professor Palmer, "cannot be equated with technique. It comes from the integrity of the teacher, from his or her relation to subject and students, from the capricious chemistry of it all."[6]

I hope I understand. Professor McKale's comments, questions, and explanations on returned exams and papers, for example, were as carefully written and revealingly pithy as were his lectures. He was just; he was fair to his students. He knew his subject. He knew his students, and he drew them into conversation. No doubt about it, good teaching is hard work. For many of us who worked with Professor McKale education became what it should ideally be. The semester's work was no longer a matter of earning a grade. What became important was learning and gaining as much as possible in a limited amount of time.

Though he was quick to point out in private a student's "lazy" effort (e.g., lack of accuracy and precision or poor writing), Professor McKale was even quicker to acknowledge and to congratulate a job well done. He inspired us all to try. If he demanded anything of us it was that we genuinely work to reach a higher plateau. What we learned from him was something that Richard W. Paul, Director of the Center for Critical Thinking and Moral Critique, has stated:

> People become educated, as against trained, insofar as they learn to think for themselves; to gather, analyze, synthesize, and assess what is presented to them for belief. Education is not a mere piling up of more and more bits and pieces of information. It is a process of deciding for ourselves what to believe and do. It implies a self-motivated action upon our own thinking and a participation in the forming of our own character. It is a process in which we learn to open our mind, to correct and refine it, to enable it to rule over its own knowledge, to gain command over its own faculties, to achieve flexibility, fairmindedness, and critical exactness.[7]

Most importantly, Professor McKale, unlike many learned people, did not dwell on our inadequacies and youthful ignorances. Instead, he showed to us our capabilities and potentialities and revealed to us a world full of possibility. In the going, we learned to gain our hopes, or at least to fulfill our needs in trying. As Professor Palmer has remarked, "good teaching requires courage—the courage to expose one's ignorance as well as insight, to invite contradiction as well as consent, to yield some control in order to empower the group, to evoke other people's lives as well as reveal one's own."[8]

Professor McKale's knowledge and guidance were not restricted to the classroom. Often he could be found talking to us in hallways, in the library, at special events, or even on the basketball court. He made us feel welcome to come to him for advice. He turned away no student in need; he was available to us all. Those of us who have known him realize that an eyebrow raised in a certain manner, or a frown, conveyed more than words ever could when Professor McKale was a bit disappointed.

A rare breed was the person who would not work long, hard hours to please him. But we all knew that, just as he frowned, Professor McKale smiled more often, and that he gave congratulatory winks, and encouraging pats on the back. For most of us, any of these recognitions of a job well done was enough to give us courage and the determination to work even harder.

When all was said and done, Professor McKale really demanded nothing of us; we had to decide for ourselves whether to learn or not to learn. He motivated us. We wanted to learn. Once that decision was made by us, Professor McKale hoped for a great deal from us, and he deserved it. But what was his secret!

It is easy to understand why I find such courage and comfort in remembering my experiences as a student with Professor McKale. The good news is that he is still teaching at Clemson University. We keep in touch by phone, letters, visits. To this day I'm still reading books with him and asking countless questions. What is marvelous is that so many other people have had an opportunity to "live the mystery" with him as I first did in 1979. Whether they be students, faculty or administrators, I think our society should cherish people who care enough to ask tough questions about the state of education in our country. Thank goodness for people who force us to face ourselves and hard questions. Educators who "take heart" need more support.

Parker Palmer has summed the matter up nicely. "We need institutional support in response to that question—workshops and institutes on teaching, promotion and tenure policies that reward good teaching as handsomely as good research. But we need even more to do the inner work that good teaching demands. 'Taking heart' to teach well is a profoundly inward process, and there is no technique or reward that will make it happen."[9] However, institutional support and admirable role models go a long way in giving us the courage to "take heart."

So, this year when someone voices yet again those confounding, sometimes frightening questions (e.g. "Who cares about the past?" "Why study history?"), I'll be ready. I'll "take heart" and try to show that we cannot understand adequately, or meaningfully, the world in which we live without knowledge of the past. After all, the study of history is the study of the totality of human experience. It is through this study and eventual understanding of past human experiences in all of its complexities and its continuities and changes, that human beings can be properly introduced to the world in which we live. We cannot know where we are and who we are unless we know where we have been and what we have done. William H. McNeill, former President of the American Historical Association, responded to the question "Why study History?" years ago in his now famous pamphlet of the same title. Studying history broadens our awareness of ourselves and of humanity past and present. As Professor McNeill explained it, "we can only know ourselves by knowing how we resemble and how we differ from others. Acquaintance with the human past is the only way to such self knowledge."[10]

Over the years I have learned that my approach to teaching varies from semester to semester. Indeed, my approach often changes from course to course within a given semester. Forever I am seeking to improve my teaching performance in order to become a more effective educator. So many vital factors (e.g., the personalities and abilities of enrolled students, the subject matter, the course level) interplay to determine which approaches are most effective in any given circumstance. Regardless of the variables, I have always made every effort to be thoroughly prepared and to make use of a variety of teaching approaches designed to engage my students. Above all, I want my students to feel a part of what is taking place and to assume responsibility for their role in this process of education. Only then does learning become truly meaningful.

I have learned valuable lessons from friends, students, and colleagues about this sometimes perplexing, somewhat precarious profession of ours. Indeed, it is a quixotic quest we pursue. But it is my life, and I assume wholeheartedly the vocation's responsibilities. If nothing else, I have learned that the older I grow (and the more bald I become) the more weary I grow of hearing myself talk. Though I still offer my students lectures about particular topics and historical developments, I also make use of other approaches (e.g., guest speakers, audio-visual aids, student presentations, seminar sessions) to coax my students into being more courageous about the pursuit of knowledge. To engage them, I ask them to complete a variety of course projects, participate in both structured and unstructured discussions, and make sure that they think about what they are reading and hearing inside and outside of the classroom.

My goal is to engage all of my students in the story of the human achievement—its glories and its tragedies. In short, I try to treat my students the way Professor McKale treated us. I want to give to my students what Professor McKale gave to me. Regardless of the subject matter, I strive to lecture with vigor, a sense of scholarly fairness, and a rationally guided feeling that challenges the brightest students to think, to seek more information, and at the same time allows even the least accomplished student to understand. I want to include them all and make them all feel their part in the human story. My endeavor is never to exclude anyone from any semester's journey through the past. I want to encourage my students to participate in discussions, to not be afraid to question my evidence and conclusions, to challenge my ideas, and, most of all, to listen closely and to think.

I urge my students to try to reach a higher plateau. I prefer not to dwell on their inadequacies and youthful ignorances. As someone once wrote, "It isn't their fault that they were born after us." I like to try to show to them their capabilities and potentialities and reveal to them a world full of possibilities.

My pal Sedric Sweat, a student majoring in engineering at The University of South Carolina, said something quite pertinent one day while we were talking in between basketball games at the gym. Sedric remarked, "It's simple. Good teachers treat students like people. Students are people too." Sedric is so right. Students have names. They have faces. And they should be treated just as respectfully and humanely as any other human being living around the globe.

But still, even with all of this the question remains. What is good teaching? How does one know when one has been truly effective in having a "positive impact" on students? This is difficult to know and still more difficult to judge. The unseen and the unsaid are often much more important than the seen and the heard. How can we determine when hearts and minds have touched? In short, I am far more comfortable writing and talking about the students who have made a difference in my life than I am in claiming to have made a difference in any of their lives. One of my greatest worries is that my students will not really know, after all is said and done, how important they are to me. What can make them believe that they are, as we know, the heart of our vocation? Good teaching is "living the mystery" about which Professor Palmer has written. Certainly, it's all a mystery to me. And I intend to keep living it.

For those of us who have accompanied Professor McKale through undergraduate courses or have taken part in his graduate seminars, mere applause somehow seems inadequate return for all that he has continued to give to his students semester after semester. Good mentors are hard to find. They are worth their weight in gold. And higher education today needs more mentors who are golden. Professor McKale has influenced students from all walks of life and a variety of disciplines, and all of them have been in one degree or another touched by his knowledge, his kindness, and his concern. His pedagogical skills and his good-hearted personality are worthy of emulation.

In an effort to give him something in return for his gifts to us, those who have known him can only strive to reach his level of accomplishment and to carry with us forever to others, with conviction, the courage, dignity, hope, and faith in humanity that Professor McKale has so generously given to us, his students, through his stories of humanity's past. Having lived the mystery with Professor McKale allows me to believe that I understand what Professor Parker Palmer means when he talks and writes about good teaching being a matter of "taking heart" and "giving heart." So, what is good teaching? "Good teaching," writes Professor Palmer, "is an act of generosity, a whim of the wanton muse, a craft that grows with practice and always risky business. It is to speak plainly, a maddening mystery."[11] But I'm not worried. Until I figure it all out, I'm taking heart and giving as much of it as I can.

Notes

1. S. D. Brookfield (1990) writing in *The Skillful Teacher*, 2, and cited in *The Teaching Professor* (1991) 5(6), 2.

2. Palmer, P. (1990) Good teaching: A matter of living the mystery. *Change 22*, 16.

3. Ibid., 14.

4. Ibid., 12.

5. Ibid., 12.

6. Ibid., 11.

7. R. W. Paul in writing about the value of critical thinking in a brochure promoting a conference sponsored by the Center for Critical Thinking and Moral Critique.

8. Op. cit., Palmer, 16.

9. Ibid., 16.

10. W. H. McNeill writing in his popular pamphlet titled "Why study history?" published by The American Association of Historians.

11. Op. cit., Palmer, 11.

Teaching Students, Not Courses

Thomas P. Kasulis (Philosophy and Religion)
*Northland College**

At an academic conference on teaching, I was asked by a colleague I had just met, "I see from your name card that you are from Northland College. What do you teach?" For some perverse reason, I did not give my usual response of "philosophy and comparative religion." Instead, I simply said, "Students." After a moment's silence, my interlocutor laughed and said, "Of course, you teach students. I mean what subject do you teach?" A bit embarrassed by my own abruptness, I was happy to move on to something more like a normal conversation between two professors from small liberal arts colleges.

Later, however, I started to reflect on what had happened. Why had I responded as I originally did? What was the source of my uneasiness? As a philosopher, and even more as a student of Zen Buddhism, I know that our most off-handed comments often reveal our hidden presuppositions. Examining those presuppositions, Socrates said, is what makes life worth living. Fathoming them, the Zen Buddhist believes, is the way to enlightenment. So, I will try here to reflect on the assumptions behind my own teaching. I do this not to preach or to claim any universal significance to what I do. I do it as an exercise in self-reflection and evaluation.

---

* Prof. Kasulis is now a faculty member at Ohio State University.

1. When it comes to college teaching, it is useful to forget much of what we learned in graduate school.

A tragedy of higher education is that the licensing agency for college teachers is the university doctoral program. Many have been dismayed that most graduate programs include virtually no training in teaching. Even that observation is off the mark, however. We do learn about teaching in graduate programs. We see poor teachers who are good researchers get tenure and we see good teachers who are not stellar researchers lose their jobs. We learn the professional jargon of the trade so that we, too, talk about teaching "loads" and "release time" for research. We learn that the idea of the seminar is to have a group of graduate students read papers to each other where only the paper determines the grade for the course; class participation is irrelevant.

At its best, graduate training can have the excitement of apprenticeship, of learning the ropes from the masters in one's field. Still, many students enter graduate schools because they want to be professors, not scholars. Yet, they learn quickly that graduate school is not about teaching; it is about learning the tools of research. Often the best teachers in a university have the least contact with graduate students.

In graduate school, therefore, we often study our subject with an eye to what is of interest to the specialist and not necessarily to what can broaden a person's intellectual horizons. Graduate school may give us the academic background to teach a subject but not necessarily to teach it as part of the liberal arts. The translation of content from the graduate program to the undergraduate classroom is not an easy one. Even more importantly, however, graduate training focuses almost exclusively on content. This brings us to the next point.

2. Learning in the classroom involves not only content, but also group process and personalities.

When I starting teaching, I prepared for my classes much the way I had prepared for them as a graduate student: I went through the reading carefully, took notes, referred to secondary references, and set up what I considered to be the list of main issues. Like most new teachers, I over-prepared for the content of the class and found I ran out of time before I could cover even a third of what I had planned. Still, that was reassuring. I knew how much more I knew than the students, and it made me feel needed.

As I matured in my teaching, however, I began to realize that teaching is not simply the transferral of content. Success cannot be measured solely by "covering the material." There are at least two other dimensions to the classroom: group process and personalities. As the teacher, I am responsible for how the group interrelates. Do I encourage them to talk to me or to each other? In a lecture do I use their questions and comments to direct my attention or only as a foil to break up the monotony of my talking all the time? In seminars do I let—or, even worse, encourage—some students to dominate our discussions? How well do I direct the rhythms of the class, going back and forth between the general and the specific, the humorous and the serious, the technical and the practical?

Similarly, in asking myself how well I know my material, how often do I also ask how well I know my students? Do I know their individual strengths and weaknesses? Which student is most confident in which situation? Which most hesitant? Do I take these factors into consideration when I teach in the classroom as well as when I see the students individually during my office hours?

In preparing for class, I increasingly try to take these factors into consideration. I ask myself not only what I feel I need to cover, but also in what way. I try to imagine different scenarios of how a discussion might go. What topic might become too ponderous or which student might get lost or deeply involved? After a class is over, I try to take note not only of where we left off in terms of content, but also of how the class dynamics went and who said or did what. In short, I do what is necessary to plan to teach a class, not take one. I am no longer a graduate student; I am a professor. That involves broader responsibilities and different kinds of preparation.

3. Curricular development cannot be separated from faculty and student development.

As college teachers, we often find ourselves involved in curricular renewal. At the least, we go through and revamp the syllabi from our own courses. Very often, however, we also find ourselves participating in a campus-wide discussion about changing the curriculum as a whole. I have learned that there is no real curricular change without an accompanying change in faculty and student attitudes. Once again, there is the danger of content becoming our sole focus. We design a new curriculum, laboring months and months over its integrity, relevance, and comprehensiveness. Yet, if that process involves no change in the faculty's or the students' expectations, the change will remain superficial. Again, as professionals trained in graduate schools, we feel most comfortable and most professional when we address the content of our classroom experience. At the same time, however, we must address the attitudes and assumptions we teachers and students bring to that classroom.

In evaluating my own course and in thinking how I might change it again, I try to look not only at the content of what I teach, but also how I teach it. Could the very same materials be handled in the classroom in a different way? Furthermore, when I think about a student who had trouble with my course last time, I try not to be defensive. Of course, I cannot "change the course for one student," but can I build in some flexibility so that another student with similar learning patterns might be able to do better? Might I find a way of identifying such a student earlier in the course than I did last time? This discussion leads to a further point about teaching evaluation.

4. The only teaching evaluation that makes a real difference is self-evaluation.

This is not to minimize the value of student or peer evaluations. In analyzing my own performance, such evaluations give invaluable information. Yet, in the end, I know that I have to evaluate myself. Imagine two professors who read student evaluations saying that "this course is too hard." We all know some teachers will take that comment as an object of pride ("I don't want to be loved; I want to be respected"). Others, however, will see it as a challenge to rethink pedagogical techniques. At best, I think we must try to be honest with ourselves. What am I trying to accomplish in this course? Where did those goals come from: Myself? the students? the "tradition?" How do I justify the adjustments I have made in it over the years? What aspects of this course are the hardest for me to teach? Why? How have I set the priorities for what is important? Do I test the students on what is most important? Do I let them know what I am trying to do so that their expectations and mine may mesh?

I suspect the best way to make teachers better is to get them to talk with each other about teaching. If we make teaching the subject matter of our analysis, we will necessarily begin to value it. After all, if there is one thing college professors are good at, it is the analysis of content. We could not have gotten through graduate school without that skill. Even institutions which do not place an emphasis on publishing research can at least require its faculty to research their own personal teaching: to collect data, to do background reading, to present ideas to colleagues, and so forth. This brings me to my last point.

5. *The distinction between the liberal arts and vocationalism can easily obscure as much as it illuminates.*

Let us start with a couple of obvious points that we typically overlook. First, let us not be too critical of our students' vocationalism. They want to earn a decent living doing something they like. For us professors in the liberal arts to criticize that view is not only futile, but hypocritical. We talk about reading a poem or doing an experiment out of the pure love of the enterprise itself, not because it is useful for making a living. Who are we when we say that? Professors—people who make a living out of reading a poem or doing an experiment. Contrary to our claim that the liberal arts has nothing to do with vocationalism, we have made the liberal arts our vocation. Students know we get paid to do what we like doing. They only ask for the same chance.

Our hypocrisy deserves a sheepish smirk. Yes, we must be more careful about how we talk about the purity of education to our students. There is a darker side to the hypocrisy, however. By the fact that we are professional liberal artists, we run the risk of teaching our students as if they should be such professionals as well. It is disappointing how often we judge the success of our department's program by the number of majors it serves or by the number we sent on to graduate school last year. How exactly is teaching English as preparation for graduate school any different from teaching accounting as preparation for the CPA exam? No, it would seem more likely we should judge the success of our program in a liberal arts college by seeing how many non-majors take our courses as pure electives, not as a requirements for some major, minor, or general education program.

This brings us to the core of liberal arts education and its purpose. Some people today want to reduce the liberal arts to "cultural literacy," the familiarity with an extensive list of facts and references (including the names of major Italian Renaissance painters but not, of course, the names of the Teenage Mutant Ninja Turtles). Some portray it as the exposure to a broad sampling of different disciplines, each presented as a distilled survey of what you would learn in detail if you were a major. Some conceive it as the acquisition of a set of skills that can be tested. Some see it as the common experience in a core set of integrated courses. Each of these visions has its positive points. What they all have in common, however, is that they conceive of a liberal arts education as the content of a curriculum. As education, however, it is not a subject matter but an event, an event with content to be sure but also with group processes and individual personalities.

When we recognize that a liberal arts education is to be self-reflective about all three dimensions of education, we realize that its goal is not just to respect classics, but also to respect the diversity of other people, starting with the students in the class. It is not just to broaden our minds, but to broaden the circle of our friends. It is not just to learn critical skills, but also to use those skills within a group in a constructive way. When the liberal arts professor starts to reflect on the meaning of teaching, the meaning of liberal arts also becomes more clear. Teaching is not an occupation. It is not even a vocation. It is a style of life. In teaching others, we teach ourselves. In teaching students, we teach teachers.

A Personal Reflection on Teaching as a Career

Janet Griffin (History)
Our Lady of the Lake University

There are some professions as old as humankind itself and teaching is one of these. Plato, in many of his *Dialogues*, discusses the role of the teacher, various methods of teaching, and the role of the learner.[1] In the *Republic* (Book VII), he compares a search for knowledge which leads one from a cave of darkness and ignorance to the light of understanding. Thus, it is the role of the educator to lead a person to a deeper understanding of the human condition.

I was attracted to the teaching profession because basically it deals with people. Also, teaching is a vehicle which liberates people from the oppression of ignorance and thus they are enabled to reach new heights in accord with their human dignity. For me, teaching has been a career consonant with Gospel values and a way to personally bring the "good news" to generations of students. Besides this, I welcomed the intellectual stimulation involved in preparing courses and in pursuing scholarship through research.

My background is founded in the liberal arts tradition both on graduate and undergraduate levels. It was while engaged in these educational endeavors, I discovered I had a talent for teaching and this talent was coupled with a love of teaching which has imbued my profession for more than twenty-five years. During this time, I have taught in junior high schools, in community colleges, and at the university level. I have had experience with undergraduates as well as graduates, have taught week-end college students, and have team taught courses with colleagues. At present I am involved with developing courses in Women's Studies.

All of these educational activities have been influenced by a definite philosophy of education. Basically, I see the object of education as leading students to the fulfillment of human life through the enlargement and deepening of meaning.[2] Philip Phenix, in his work *Realms of Meaning: A Philosophy of the Curriculum for General Education* elaborates on this idea by stating that "Human beings are essentially creatures who have the power to experience meanings. Distinctively human existence consists in a pattern of meanings."[3] I, as a teacher, have sought to give meaning to the lives of my students, and one way I have accomplished this is to make my teaching student-centered: to recognize the inherent worth of each person in my classes. Specifically, I have tried to motivate my students to have a constant thirst for learning and thus gain in meaningfulness for their daily lives. This thirst, I believe, is unlimited, and my job as an educator is to motivate students to excel beyond their own expectations or as one of my professors put it: "to constantly stretch students beyond their personal limits."[4]

Closely allied with imparting meaningfulness is imparting values. There is much discussion about the role of values education, but I agree with Bruce Kimball who says the new liberal studies curriculum calls for the inculcation of values.[5] It has been a challenge to instill a definite set of Christian values while at the same time remaining open to and tolerant of diverse points of view in the classroom.

A valid philosophy of education is built around expertise in subject matter. For me, the teaching of history centers around concepts rather than mere facts. True history, since it is the story of people, involves relationships and interconnectedness. By using organized lectures, small group sharing, and oral as well as written assignments, I have led students through critical thinking to perceive these relationships and relate them to their own experiences. It is then that optimal learning takes place as Zelda Gamson observes: "When linkage is established and diversity introduced, students come to see that they can make what they learn their own. They become, in a word, committed to learning and its uses."[6] In all assignments, I have demanded high standards of performance by the students and to me it is a matter of justice to return their papers at the next class meeting.

Overall, the classroom experiences include a variety of methods with a proper use of audio visual materials. One ingredient for making these methods effective is a good sense of humor. I feel that my sense of humor has enhanced my teaching efforts and improved the learning atmosphere for my students.

Actual practices in the classroom follow a basic pattern of dividing the course into five or six major topics. For each topic I give the students a "module" or assignment sheet which lists the behavioral objectives and learning activities peculiar to that topic. Each topic is covered through lectures accompanied by an outline on the overhead projector, a quiz on a particular chapter from the text, a specific assignment to be graded (written or oral), and a test. The assigned activities vary from topic to topic and include simulation exercises, small group presentations, library research and book reviews; the last assignment is a list of comprehensive questions which cover the whole course and from which two essay questions on the final exam are chosen.

The above process is used mainly in survey and non-advanced courses. For upper division courses the learning activities are more challenging as they include an analysis of journal articles and oral reports on personalities or events covered in the topic; the individual oral reports are critiqued by other students in the class. In addition, comparisons of the views of the author of the text and other reputable historians are assigned. Because of the variety of assignments, monotony is avoided and student interest is maintained.

Teaching effectiveness is also promoted by the university administration. A university-wide activity gives recognition to students who have excelled in their classes. Two students from each class are chosen by the professor to present a paper at the Student Conference on Scholarship. This activity gives students a goal to work toward and is a strong motivating force for excellence. It is also very rewarding to the teacher.

The administration also fosters teaching excellence in two other ways. The University's "Statement of Purpose" contains the following dictum: "In all academic programs, good teaching has the highest priority . . ."[7] This is implemented by the fact that the administration sponsors a "Faculty Idea Exchange" with a full day of sharing by the faculty on effective teaching techniques and experiences. The Academic Dean further reinforces good teaching by writing a congratulatory letter to each faculty member who receives high scores on student evaluation forms. These administrative activities are very affirming to faculty members and serve as motivation for greater teacher excellence.

All the teaching methods in the world cannot be effective unless there is a good relationship between teacher and student. I feel I have had a positive impact in the classroom because of my concern and interest in each student as an individual. This interest has been shown by my enthusiasm for the topic being taught and by my availability to students outside the classroom. I take a special interest in those students needing extra help and I initiate a conference with them to assist in the learning process. Interest and concern are also provided by a disciplined atmosphere for optimal learning. I give grading criteria and requisites for each course on the first day of the semester and these are clear and concise. I encourage students to challenge my ideas and I allow them to test their own mistakes and diverse views throughout the course. I further challenge the more gifted students by requiring extra work over and above the regular assignments for those working toward an "A" or a "B" in a course. All in all, the classroom atmosphere I have tried to build and maintain is based upon one component of the educational philosophy of Our Lady of the Lake University from its Statement of Purpose: We, the students and I, are a community of learners.[8]

Having discussed my role as a teacher, I now will consider the role of teaching within a liberal arts setting in higher education. Quality teaching is essential to the success of liberal arts programs. Much has been written about the constitutive elements of the liberal arts curriculum, but no definitive conclusion seems to have been reached. Yet, all scholars seem to agree upon the importance of first rate teachers within the realm of liberal arts. Improved teaching is one of the demands of the proponents of the "new liberal education."[9] The importance of teaching is also borne out by the fact that a major seminar in the Lilly Endowment Workshop on the Liberal Arts was entitled "The Art of Teaching."[10] Effective teaching gives life to any curriculum and it is especially necessary for imparting the liberal arts, as Elof Carlson observes:

> If the liberal arts are not simply found in a set of books or times past or needs present, how can we teach them? We need look no further than ourselves. We all can recognize the good in ourselves and in others. We can distinguish the true from opinion and false leads through our scholarly habits, and we can appreciate the many forms of beauty that all societies revere in diverse ways.[11]

The liberally educated person described by Carlson is one who has acquired the "best habits of humanity," and it is through the liberal arts that one learns to listen, to care, and to act.[12] Only first rate teachers can prepare students to be receptive to such humane characteristics.

At a teacher education college, professors have the privilege and duty not only to teach liberal arts subjects, but to personify liberal arts values. We teach with our whole person and we are models for our students in our critical, analytical, and reflective approaches. These characteristics are intangibles which we pass on to our students who will one day be teachers and hopefully imbue their students with the values inherent in the liberal arts. These results, however, will not be achieved without skillful and well prepared teachers.

In specific terms, the teaching of history plays a key role in any liberal arts curriculum. History provides the students with a background against which they can make their own choices, and it enables them to become "aware of how they and history intersect."[13] Thus, the student in relating ideas from other disciplines learns what it means to be human, a goal of any liberally educated person.

I realize that many of my personal reflections in this paper may be interpreted as idealistic and I hasten to add that not all of my attempts at teaching have been successful. On the whole, however, I have been blessed with success in teaching, and I am happy I took the risk of committing myself to teaching, a profession which has paid rich dividends in personal growth coupled with much joy. I look forward to the distinct challenges which the next twenty-five years will bring.

Notes

1. Plato's treatment of teaching can be found in the following: *Apology, Republic* (Book I), *Protagoras, Meno, Symposium,* and *Phaedrus.* These works served as texts for a seminar "The Art of Teaching" led by H. Sinaiko at the Lilly Endowment Workshop on the Liberal Arts, at Colorado College, June 15–29, 1991.

2. Phenix, P. H. (1964), *Realms of meaning: A philosophy of the curriculum for general education.* New York: McGraw-Hill, 5.

3. Ibid., 5.

4. Blake, J. H. (1991). "Reflections on liberal education," Lilly Endowment Workshop on the Liberal Arts, Colorado College, June 15-29, 2.

5. Kimball, B. A. (1991). "Curricular implications of the recent knowledge revolution: Rediscovering the new liberal education," Lilly Endowment Workshop on the Liberal Arts, (Colorado College, June 15–29), 14. A slightly different approach to values in education can be found in Thomas M. Landry (1990). "Lay leadership in Catholic higher education: Where will it come from?" *America, 162,* 264–267.

6. Gamson, Z. F., *et al.* (1984). "What should liberal education mean?" in *Liberating Education.* San Francisco: Jossey-Bass, 50.

7. *Undergraduate Bulletin* 1991–93. San Antonio, Texas: Our Lady of the Lake University, 8.

8. Ibid., 8.

9. Op. cit., 4-5. Medical schools also are stressing the importance of a liberal arts approach to education. See "Physicians for the Twenty-First Century," Association of American Medical Colleges. For a review of literature on

the history of liberal education and a survey of its meaning, see B. A. Kimball (1986). *Orators and Philosophers.* New York: Columbia University. For an analysis of the state of liberal education in the 80s, see Z. F. Gamson (1984). "What Should Liberal Education Mean," in *Liberating Education.* San Francisco: Josey-Bass.

10. H. Sinaiko, seminar "The Art of Teaching" at the Lilly Endowment Workshop on the Liberal Arts, at Colorado College, June 15–29, 1991.

11. Carlson, E. A. (1991). "Teaching and the Liberal Arts," paper delivered at the Lilly Endowment Workshop on the Liberal Arts, Colorado College, June 15–29, 8.

12. Ibid., 4,7.

13. Op. cit., Gamson, 25.

Learning as Conversation

Patricia O'Connell Killen (Religion)
Dennis M. Martin (English)
Pacific Lutheran University

> To teach is to create a space where the community of truth can be practiced with passion and discipline.—*Parker Palmer*

> Real conversation occurs only when the participants allow the question, the subject matter, to assume primacy. It occurs only when our usual fears about our own self-image die: whether that fear is expressed in either arrogance or scrupulosity matters little. That fear dies only because we are carried along, and sometimes away, by the subject matter itself into the rare event or happening named "thinking" and "understanding." For understanding happens; it occurs not as the pure result of personal achievement but in the back-and-forth movement of the conversation itself.—*David Tracy*

The two questions posed to us for this essay—what is behind our effectiveness as teachers and what is the role of first-rate teaching in liberal arts colleges—imply a prior and critical question: what are the dynamics and significance of human beings coming to know anything? Or to put it even more fundamentally: how do human beings come to understanding and why should they bother?

Sociologist turned educator, Parker Palmer, captures the answer compactly: significant understanding happens in "a community of truth practiced with passion and discipline." Palmer sees truth as interactive. One encounters it in a community of people who combine affective engagement with skillful practice in their common commitment to discovering truth.

Theologian David Tracy carries Palmer's definition further with his description of genuine conversation. Tracy also accents the participants' engagement with subject matter and their ability to blend affective commitment and intellectual rigor. He describes a conversation that is collaborative, not competitive. As participants share their curiosity, knowledge, and ignorance with each other, they all benefit. Because of the common commitment to the pursuit of understanding and meaning, the interpersonal dynamics in the group are respected. Not individualistic ego gratification and power building, but the stimulation, challenge, and sheer joy of coming to understand are the rewards of Tracy's kind of conversation.

Engaging in genuine conversation with oneself, with one's subject matter, with other human beings, and with one's wider social context is how learning happens. Artful teachers self-consciously create a context in which genuine conversation happens and engage their students in that conversation. Even more, they cultivate in students the habits, skills, and qualities of mind necessary to engage in such conversation.

While the context for genuine conversation will have a different tone, texture, and subject content depending on the course, students, and instructors, there are three characteristics of such classroom contexts which we believe are identifiable across disciplinary lines. The first is a teacher's willingness and ability to model and mentor being a competent learner as much, or more than, an expert knower. The second is a teacher's introducing, and sequentially illustrating, thinking and reasoning skills of growing complexity that are then practiced by students, built upon in the class, and employed by students in their assignments. The third is the practice of regularly stopping to explore the human significance of everything that is being learned. This essay reflects on these elements of creating a context for genuine conversation in the classroom out of our experience of team-teaching.

Each spring semester we team-teach an Integrated Studies course to freshmen. The course completes the two-semester foundational sequence built on the theme of change for the

137

alternative core curriculum at Pacific Lutheran University. Its focus is on the dynamics of change in the period from the Enlightenment to World War I. Both the historical period and the theme allow considerable latitude in terms of course content and approach. In designing and teaching the course, our aim of creating a context for and building students' abilities to engage in genuine conversation guides us.

Genuine conversation is not friendly banter or serial talking. In our case it involves two teachers and thirty or so students, each reaching across the spaces that surround an isolated self to make connections with each other, with the material, and with their times. Making fruitful connections is not easy. In an interdisciplinary course such as ours we and the students must integrate material and concepts from history, literature, religious studies, economics, and sociology. We and the students must abstract from massive amounts of material to pull out key concepts, to begin to notice patterns, to organize ideas, events, and interpretations. As teachers we support students experiencing the frustration and fear that go with facing the ambiguity of interpretation. We send students back to the text repeatedly as we coax them to engage and not just read. Finally, we ask that they sit and interact with material until they develop original positions and ideas.

Creating the context for genuine conversation in a course such as ours requires that the teachers forego the role of expert knower and take up more explicitly the role of competent learner. Our teaching is grounded in our common knowledge that our students are persons, in our commitment to their learning, and in our shared intellectual curiosity. In our teaching, we draw on the energy generated by our sense of discovery, and on the breadth as much as the depth of our human experience and reading. What authority we have in our classroom flows from our constant demonstration that we value what we are learning and that we want students to know how to learn as we do. We do not take for granted that we have an exclusive competence: we re-establish our competence everyday.

We are able to ground our teaching in energetic intellectual curiosity and the desire to continue to be learners because we teach in a university in which teaching excellence is valued, in which administrative structures exist to bring us together out of our respective departments, and because creation of new, specialized knowledge is not forced upon us as the exclusive or even the primary goal of our professional work. When, for example, one of us decides to study opera as an integrated form of art and to bring scenes from operas into our classroom, the learning that person does is institutionally valued and supported even though it is not likely to lead to professional publication.

We would argue, however, that even in primarily research-oriented schools teaching has to be grounded in energetic intellectual curiosity and the willingness of teachers to hold themselves as learners. Without these groundings teaching becomes the passing on of knowledge from those who have it to those who do not. Our experience is that too often those who receive it have no idea what to do with it or why they ought to extend themselves in knowing it. There is no conversation. Significant scholars in all fields embody energetic intellectual curiosity and are always learners in their research areas. Teaching aimed at genuine conversation requires that those qualities be translated into the undergraduate classroom.

There is rigor to building genuine conversation in the humanities. It is not easy for the students or us because the liberating arts of integrating, abstracting, garnering creative threads in ambiguity, and articulating original positions are just that, arts. Persons are formed as much as educated into these arts. They entail much more than students' mastery of the ability to repeat, analyze, and synthesize material. Those skills, practiced separately from commitment to and care for the subject matter and for our world, are the techniques of shriveled human beings. We are training students to be reflective human beings, persons in whom passion and critical acumen combine for richness of life.

Our aim, nurturing reflective human beings through genuine conversation, is ambitious. A number of variables contribute to our success or failure. The outcome rests on our ability to relate students to the material, and the material to students, in ways that open up both. It rests on the willingness of students and ourselves to enter into the back-and-forth of genuine conversation. This requires that we and they bring some depth of personal integrity into the classroom and maintain it in situations of conflict, confusion, and hard work. Success rests on our mastery of the disciplines that we teach and our willingness to translate the material and methods of those disciplines for our students. It also rests on students' willingness to commit to mastering course material which means more than going through the motions of reading the assigned chapters. Success rests on our and the students' willingness to let authority belong to the voice of wisdom in the conversation, not to the role of designated teacher or most vocal student in the room. In short, creating a context of genuine conversation in the classroom requires attending to the learning process in the classroom as much as to the material in the syllabus.

Team-teaching provides significant advantages to persons who view education as we do. First a word on what we mean by team-teaching. Team-teaching as commonly practiced seems to us to be modeled on the concept of a relay team, with one teacher always in the center. We could call it serial teaching. In the worst cases of this style, the teacher not in the center does not even do the assignments or come to class when he or she is not at the center that day. This model presumes that one's teaching is grounded in one's professional disciplinary expertise. Authority flows, in such a classroom, from a superior command of information and technique.

Our teaching resembles another kind of team, doubles tennis, where both partners are in play all the time, with specific roles constantly changing in reaction to the situation, to what others in play are saying and doing. We practice team-teaching as a continuous partnership through the semester. We are up together each day. Neither one is the official expert on the material of a particular discipline or text. Together we have worked through the material before we go to class; have a sense of the direction the class period might go; have identified the learning goals for the day; and, know the three or so ways we might move toward those goals depending on the process of the group. After class we discuss our perceptions of what happened, what worked, what did not work, why, and where we might go next.

140

In the classroom, team-teaching provides the opportunity to teach in slow motion. We cannot both speak at the same time. This makes us each more careful about what we will say; words are precious and need to be precise and incisive. Since we cannot both be talking at the same time, the silent one listens and observes the learning process of students. That listening and observation occasions new ideas or strategies for questioning or giving brief input. The back-and-forth of our presenting and questioning and conversing with students allows us to translate each other's material for students when it is helpful. As well, the slow-motion provided by team-teaching makes it possible for one of us to remind both partner and students why we are doing what we are doing at any given time, to note shifts in the level of abstraction of questions or analysis, and to summarize key points in a discussion. In short, team-teaching gives us each more time to think while in the teaching process.

Team-teaching as we do it has a direct affect on the question of authority in the classroom, an issue crucial to our view of learning as participating in genuine conversation. Ours is a decentered classroom. It has become common recently to speak of a decentered classroom as one which breaks cleanly from the tradition of formal lecture. In most contexts, the image this term brings to mind is of a teacher setting up small-group discussions, panel presentations, and student-originated projects. The teacher in such a classroom deliberately withdraws from the center of attention and authority in order to share power with the students.

We team-teach a course which, in contrast to this image, never has a center, no single voice of authority from which knowledge flows. In our classroom, two voices are heard in conversation, first with each other, then increasingly with student voices as they join the conversation.

From the beginning of the course we agreed that neither of us would occupy and speak from the center-front of the classroom. Instead we took positions one to the right and one to the left of center. We both move around in front of the classroom. One writes on the board as the other speaks. We both pace out the size of an apartment for a family of ten in industrial Birmingham, England, on the linoleum squares in front of the students' desks. We alternate talking and questioning. We stop for a moment to check out perceptions with each other and with students about how the learning process is working. All of this helps students to see and participate in the sharing of authority in the classroom. Authority shared by two is easily widened to authority shared by ten or fifteen or thirty.

The decentering of authority in the classroom supports our primary agenda: that students see how truth comes out of conversation, carried on with passion and discipline, not out of lecturing and listening. Information is important, so we have texts and we do lecture. Listening is important, letting in information and concepts. But truth is interactive. It involves the testing of my hearing and my information and my conceptual frameworks against the material and against the interpretations of the material by others in the class. To argue for the affective and volitional dimensions of truth is not to give in to privatism and solipsism. Rather, it is to return humanities education to where it originated: through personal and social experience in conversation with wisdom from the past.

The human base of all learning and knowing came through pointedly for us this past spring at the summarizing exercise in class. We had the students identify the three ideas that they thought mattered the most during the class. In groups they pooled their ideas and then submitted four as nominees to the class. All nominees for central ideas went up on the blackboard. Then as a class we discussed the ideas, clustered where there seemed to be patterns, and voted. We eliminated all but the top ten ideas, discussed again and voted again. By the end of the discussion we came up with three ideas which expressed our consensus of what the course had been about. This spring, using the exercise for a second year in a row, we observed something that fascinated us: for each group the themes they identified as key to understanding the years from the Enlightenment to World War I also reflected their experience of learning in the class. This year, for a group which had difficulty mastering abstraction and building their own interpretive patterns for material, the winning themes for the course were: struggle for survival— competition and class struggle; secularization—movement from supernatural to natural explana-

142

tions; and, identity of classes and individuals. In contrast, last year, for a group which had a strong sense of its own authority and often resisted all authority of the teachers, the winning nominees were freedom, power, and community. Two groups provide only anecdotal evidence. Still, the pattern we have seen calls for further observation.

Creating a context for genuine conversation often entails repetition of exercises which are second nature to the teacher. A basic rule for good teaching, however, is to overcome the second-nature quality of these skills by always trying to remember what it was like before one knew some information or had acquired an intellectual skill. That exercise in memory yields rich insight into one's own learning process, hunches about what might happen in the classroom, and clues on how to design a session or unit.

One second-nature skill of a teacher is the ability to translate new material into another frame of reference in order to increase mastery and develop critical understanding of this new material. This is a foundational skill which begins to build the higher level activities of abstraction and analysis. Most of our students are not familiar with the fundamental act of abstracting from the details of concrete experience. They can talk about their experiences while frying burgers at McDonalds. They cannot yet structure a conversation about how employers can avoid paying costly benefits by limiting workers to part-time schedules, or about how such behavior exploits a youthful or elderly work force. We find that students need to see the skills of translation, abstraction, and analysis applied time after time so they can develop them. It is not enough, we find, simply to require students to work at these levels; this would be like requiring someone to dance ballet who had never seen one.

To nurture the skills of translation, abstraction, and analysis we begin by building grids on the blackboard. Grids are simple frameworks for translating material from the way the text presented it into another reference scheme. We begin by constructing a sample grid on the board at the beginning of class on the day we start the unit on the French Revolution.

One column lists possible factors of change. The other columns divide the French Revolution into three phases as differentiated by the assigned text. Working with the class we ask about each of the factors in relation to each phase of the French Revolution. We sometimes give examples to help them begin their responses. For instance, how did Louis XVI's need for new tax revenue contribute to the Revolution? Or, what impact did a mass act such as the storming of the Bastille have on making the Revolution happen? How did an idea such as Rousseau's concept of the general will influence people? Or, how much can be attributed to the character and actions of an individual such as Napoleon? With a little demonstration and some questioning the students go on to fill out the grid. We record students' responses on the blackboard and discuss them. We also participate by adding elements that we consider significant but that they have missed.

As the students shape and publicly give answers to fill in the grid, they begin to sort and order the material they have read. They begin to abstract general principles or ideas or themes from the concrete detail of the historical narrative. They begin to make judgments and to interpret influences and forces involved in historical events. They begin to see how complex the historical reality described in the text really was and to see how that reality's appearance is colored by the interpretive frame of the author of the text, of the teachers of the class, and even their own inchoate pre-understandings about social relationships. They begin to be able to ask questions such as: Why these three demarcations for the phases of the French Revolution? What do the categories of forces of change have to do with them? What happens if we divide the periods of the French Revolution differently? How do we weigh the relative weight of the factors in explaining the causes of change in any one of the periods? The asking of such questions begins genuine conversation.

The repeated use of such grids by teachers, and then the construction of grids by students, develops their interpretive abilities. After having done grids frequently during the first part of the course, we then ask the students to create and fill in their own grids under a different name: posters. For the poster assignment we divided the class into pairs with each pair assigned a different topic: education, family, geography, technology, international relations, science, religion, literature, etc. Each pair was to do a "deep slice" of the year 1840 in relation to their assigned topic. Their task was to gather as much information as they could, sort and organize the material, and make a poster for presentation to the class. The students knew that the purpose of the assignment was, as a class, to create as full an understanding of the year 1840 in the United States as possible in order to prepare to read some Nathaniel Hawthorne stories. On "poster day" each partner spent half the class session as resource presenter for her or his poster and half the session rotating around the room learning from other posters. This made all the students experts in one area and made them all teachers. Poster days test out everyone's ability to engage in genuine conversation with material and with one's peers. Poster days also illustrate the profoundly collaborative nature of knowledge in all disciplines.

Having practiced the translation, abstraction, pattern identification, organization, and interpretive skills that are required to work grids in class discussion or to make posters, we support the students in building these skills through the test questions we assign. This year the students were given two test questions for the final exam for the course. They had a week to work on the questions individually and in groups and were given permission to bring one three-by-five note card to the exam with notes on both sides. The questions were: (1) Identify three key ideas for each of the following topics we have studied and use these ideas to discuss how cultural change happens in response to ideas: the Industrial Revolution, Romanticism, Evolution, and Imperialism. (2) Choose one person from among Nathaniel Hawthorne, Anne Lee, Karl Marx, George Bernard Shaw, or John S. Mill. Write an essay showing how this person is representative of and challenges their cultural context. Use this person as an example of how individuals contribute to cultural change.

Both questions required that students demonstrate an ability to present concrete material correctly and to organize it to support their interpretations of how ideas and individuals respectively influence cultural change. Accuracy and adequacy of concrete data were factored into the exam grade as were the demonstration of abstractive, analytic, and interpretive skills.

There is a final part of our work to create the context for genuine conversation in the classroom which we have come to believe in deeply: "Asking the 'So what?' question." We do not ask this question rudely, of course, but we do ask it persistently and when we ask it we do mean to force attention to a critical issue. "Why," we are always asking, "does this matter?" We always want to know "Who cares?" We never assume that anything we teach matters in and of itself, even though we often believe that the subject is intrinsically important: whether it be a much-studied novel such as *The Heart of Darkness*, or the distinction between Lamark's and Darwin's understanding of species change, or Weber's Protestant ethic thesis, or Wagnerian opera, we do not assume that its importance is self-evident. We ask ourselves, each other, and our students why a human being should value these things. We may know that Conrad's novel is valuable, in part, because of its complex relationship with the tradition of literary impressionism, but that value is not where we start in class. We specifically ask students about what in the text they care. Then we go ahead to suggest ways that they could care about other parts, by finding analogies in common experience to the exotic events of the novel, by drawing on our personal experiences, and by translating into terms that students can understand. Our students will go on to learn the conventions of naming and classifying that are institutionalized in academic disciplines, but first we want them to ask the hardest question, to ask and ask again, "So what?" As they continually answer that question, they repeatedly reengage in conversational learning. Answering that question prepares them to extend their knowledge to more disciplinary-determined and technical aspects of a topic.

Answering "So what?" begins the exploration of the significance of what is learned. Answering that question connects the conversation about the subject matter to the values, questions, and concerns of the people present in the classroom. Answering it focuses the cognitive, affective, and volitional energy required to explore material, to listen, to make connections, to care about the life of the mind and its implications for everyday life. It lets each one say why he or she is willing to enter the adventure of understanding, to engage in genuine conversation, with all the risks, frustrations, and joys which it involves.

Genuine conversation happens among committed participants who are willing to engage one another about a common issue with passion and discipline. They must come to honor the deeply affective energy involved in human curiosity and to accept with courage the frustration of developing the skills of intellectual rigor. Creating the context for such conversation is a new task each time our course is taught.

As we experience it, learning through conversation recalls the words of T. S. Eliot's poem, "Gerontion," where an old man looking back over the wealth of knowledge life has provided him asks, "After such knowledge, what forgiveness?" We recognize that the conversation in which we engage our students challenges them, not just to know more, but to know life more fully, life full of uncertainty and ambiguity. We try to show all our students, perhaps especially the future teachers among them, that thinking independently and critically takes personal courage. The reward to students for this courage is that all of life will be open to them and that they will not be alone.

From our own experience as learners and teachers we know that no deep and long-lasting learning happens without genuine conversation. We are convinced that without genuine conversation in the classroom, no real teachers—persons grounded in intellectual curiosity and passion for human life, persons able to suffer creatively, persons committed to the liberating engagement with the humanistic disciplines—are being formed.

Preparation for Leadership: Student-Oriented Teaching in Liberal Arts Colleges

William J. Woolley (History)
Ripon College

The editor of this volume has given authors the task of examining the "dual themes" of "effective teaching" and the role of such teaching in the liberal arts. In some respects this means examining the idea of effective teaching within the broader educational concept of the liberal arts. This is a useful approach since the two "themes" are at once both distinct and yet interrelated not only in that the second provides the context for the first, but on another plane, each helps define the other. Certain approaches to education are particularly effective in the liberal arts tradition, while that tradition may, in part, be defined by the approaches taken to teaching within it.

In fact, defining either concept separately, without discussing its relationship to the other has proven extremely difficult. Of the two terms, "effective teaching" has long been the more elusive. While "liberal arts" continues to preserve a remarkable ambiguity within a rising flood of educational discourse, a fundamental consensus does exist as to its conceptual parameters in terms of meaning, forms, and objectives. Effective teaching, on the other hand, commands no such paradigmatic consensus. In many places the term has to do with little more than instructor popularity as measured by student evaluations and recurrent nominations as "Teacher of the Year."

Attempts to go beyond this obviously nebulous and limited characterization proceed almost aimlessly in several directions. One direction is to define effective teaching in terms of the personality of the instructor with teaching success linked to character traits such as intelligence, dedication, charisma, effort, compassion, sensitivity, and imagination. Another approach tends to treat effective teaching as a function of environment looking at class size, student quality and motivation, and the resources made available for academic purposes (e.g., a computer at every desk) as the main factors behind teaching success. Yet a third approach links quality teaching with instructional style defining success in terms such as "thoroughness," "accessibility," and "rigor." Moreover, each of these approaches tends to define teaching differently and is founded on a different set of expectations of the instructor so that a simple "all of the above" becomes an impossible agglomeration that provides no useful guidance in defining effective teaching.

Such chaos is compounded by a lack of agreement as to how teaching quality is to be assessed. Student satisfaction as determined by end of semester evaluations, professional peer analyses of teaching methods and materials, and administrative evaluation of efficiency in terms of full time equivalents or of quantified analysis of exit examination results are all methods used for assessing teaching quality although, obviously, they each measure quite different things.

What this chaos demonstrates is the near impossibility of meaningfully defining effective teaching as an autonomous concept outside of a larger educational framework. On the other hand, one can produce at least an island of greater clarity in this confusion by considering the linkage between effective teaching and liberal arts education. Simplicity suggests identifying effective teaching as that particular approach to education which best achieves the objectives of the liberal arts. Reversing the equation produces the interesting idea that liberal arts education is, in part, the product of a particular approach to teaching. The linkage, in this case, however is not simply mathematics (i.e., effective teaching = liberal arts) which is in itself devoid of meaning. The two-way linkage can be understood only by examining the objectives of liberal arts education.

Given the pedagogic pluralism still existent among educational institutions claiming membership in the liberal arts community, it would be difficult to outline with any brevity the entire realm of agreed upon objectives of liberal arts education. What follows, therefore, is only a personal opinion based upon my own experience at Ripon College. It is offered as an example of how a consideration of the objectives of liberal arts education as they seem to be defined at one institution have been used by an instructor in shaping his own approach to effective teaching.

The liberal arts tradition is itself a part of the greater realm of undergraduate education and any examination of its objectives should be approached by denoting its particular place in this context. While I see the overarching goal of all undergraduate education to be the liberation of the maturing individual from a state of dependence to a state of independence, it seems to me that the purpose of liberal arts institutions, and especially quality liberal arts institutions, is to carry that objective further in terms of training their students to take eventual leadership roles in a democratic society. To prepare their students to be independent and functioning members of society, undergraduate institutions have generally seen themselves doing two things. One is to convey to their students both the knowledge necessary to become literate members of society and the skills necessary to use that knowledge in a functionally useful manner. The other is to provide them with the self-awareness and self-knowledge necessary to give them the sense of direction needed for purposeful activity and the confidence needed to proceed boldly down the paths chosen.

While most undergraduate institutions tend to put the greater part of the emphasis in their programs on the first of these two objectives, the teaching of content and skills, it seems to me that for colleges in the liberal arts tradition the second, objective, helping in the discovery of self, is by far the more important. I do agree with Lynn Cheney and others that college graduates need to have had access to a considerable body of information in order to be able to enter careers and to begin to become active participants in the life of their communities. My courses are, in fact, jammed with material to the point that they have the reputation of being both "a lot of work" and of value because one "learns a lot." Moreover, I also stress the development of learning skills and communication skills. Still, it seems to me that a well-developed awareness of one's own individuality is the cornerstone of the capacity to function as a purposeful member of a community as well as to lead an individually satisfying life. More important, perhaps, it is a clear necessity for anyone accepting leadership roles later in life. Thus in my view effective teaching in a liberal arts setting is that approach to education best suited to helping students discover and cultivate the rich potentials of their own selves and personalities. In short, it must be "student-oriented" teaching.

Student-oriented teaching is not just a cliche for the ornamentation of college admissions literature. It is a distinct approach to education with its own advantages and drawbacks and one which can be compared to other equally valid approaches to instruction such as "teacher-oriented" and "subject-oriented" education, each of which also has its own set of advantages and drawbacks. In "teacher-oriented" education or "mentoring," instructors provide their own well-considered and complexly integrated vision of the world and how it is to be understood. In "subject-oriented" education, students are provided with a distinct body of material which derives its coherence and outlook from the canons of the discipline. Students who internalize either or both of these experiences to a substantial degree will be educated persons in terms of having been acceptably socialized, having gained a wide range of useful knowledge, and having learned mature points of view, in short, everything necessary to be useful citizens in social and economic spheres.

What may be lacking in such education is the cultivation of the sense of self-knowledge and self-assurance necessary to function effectively in leadership situations which require the imagination to create ways of understanding new and confusing situations and problems, the ability to formulate effective social responses to both, and the capacity to articulate and communicate these ideas to a wider audience. This imagination, creativity, confidence, and capacity to communicate with a broader audience are functions of a well-cultivated concept of self and are best acquired by an approach to education focussed on the needs of the individual students and aimed primarily at the development of their own self-awareness and of their capacity to respond effectively to problems they encounter. This is what I would define as "student-oriented" teaching. It is, I think, uniquely suitable to liberal arts colleges and, when practiced, contributes to the distinctiveness of liberal arts education. For this reason, it may be the approach to education that would be the most "effective" in a liberal arts setting.

Student-oriented education has its drawbacks. The amount of time that must be given to the needs of the students may preclude covering all the material canonically defined by professionals in the discipline as vital to the course being taught. This could mean history without the Civil War, political science without Hobbes, art without Delacroix, or chemistry without polymers. In addition, student-oriented teaching puts great strain on the coherence of a course. A course gains its coherence by being rationally structured around the instructor's own outlook which serves as a thesis. Focussing the course on the outlooks and needs of the various students risks fragmenting that structure, atomizing the course into a melange of disparate and seemingly meaningless experiences. Hence, the coherence given to the content of a course by the canon of the discipline and the intellectual integrity provided by the outlook of the instructor cannot be ignored if the course is to retain any educational value at all. However, even accepting the value of traditional course formats, there are still many ways in which courses can be structured to focus primary emphasis on the students and their needs. How this can be done will vary enormously from school to school and from instructor to instructor. I am offering my own approach only as an example of how I do it at Ripon.

I begin by designing my courses to be sets of experiences rather than packages of knowledge. While I remain concerned with what the students will learn, my primary focus is on how they will respond since the development of an individual capacity to respond to situations is the first step toward the creation of both a genuine sense of self and a capacity to lead.

Therefore, the items that form the content of the course are chosen not so much on the basis of their own intrinsic value, but chiefly in terms of how they may be used to help students develop the ability to respond. Each class is then designed around the development of situations to which students must respond, so that one major goal of the course is to help students learn how to respond. The first step in this internal educational program is that they must learn that the key to how to respond lies within themselves rather than within any given orthodoxy. While I do stress that historians have developed highly sophisticated means of making sense of this world and that I expect students to become acquainted with these approaches to the point that they can use them, my primary emphasis is on the idea that for any given student the only "right" idea is their own idea. This does not mean that all ideas are equal. The intelligent, well-considered, and well-formulated response is always superior to the off-the-wall guess. But, while accepting that, I still try to create an atmosphere in the class friendly to imagination and competing ideas.

The form of response sought, of course, is participation rather than recitation since it is only by doing so that a person gains a sense of confidence and of self. Hence, in my courses, individual class sessions are designed to invite participation and the focus is on that participation. For this reason, along with many of my colleagues, I am slowly shifting my classes from lectures to discussions. However, I try to get the students to approach even my lectures from the position of participants rather than that of mere passive auditors. My principal means of doing this is by interrupting a lecture to ask questions that lead to a brief discussion. In this way, I emphasize that the purpose of the lecture is to provide students with material they will need for later discussion. Moreover, in my questions I often ask students to place themselves in the historical situation that I have described and suggest what they think and act out what ought to have been done. It is not too difficult for students to have an opinion about these things and one can count on these opinions being sufficiently intelligent to reflect the range of options that may actually have been considered at the time so that there are initially no wrong answers. Yet, by responding, the students gain the sense of being participants in history itself as well as being empowered to act as judges of other participants. As one of these experiences is piled upon another, students gradually begin to give up their earlier self-identification as passive dependents in favor of more activist and confident self-images.

The focus in class discussions is on the formation of opinions about things since the act of forming an opinion about an issue also pushes students into forming new opinions about themselves as well as building confidence in their capacity to make judgments. I do this in several ways. Sometimes I suggest contrasting interpretations of events and ask students which they prefer and why. I often link each initial interpretation offered by students with a specific historian so that all options are equally backed by authority. This means, again, that there are no right or wrong answers, but it also means that students can not get by on guessing but must support their opinion with reasoned argument and evidence. An alternative to this is to take note of an event and ask students to explain how it happened. Again students can be counted on to be intelligent enough to provide explanations falling within the range of interpretations normally offered by historians so that I can usually respond to any student's idea with the statement that it is in line with a well-accepted historical interpretation. As a result the students get a sense of themselves as part of a mature historical community engaged in an on-going effort to explain a development. As this sense of identity with that community grows, I gradually drop the practice of authenticating student responses by linking them with ideas of historical authorities. Instead, students are identified as the sole sponsors of their concepts and are made responsible for articulating and defending them in a mature competition of ideas. Finally, examinations and papers are structured so that students are, again, asked to form and support opinions, with the grades based on the quality of the idea and of the supporting argument and use of evidence.

Finally, it seems to me that there can be no real sense of self as a confident actor and leader without encountering real challenge. On campus I am known as a difficult teacher because I set hard problems and demand that students do them well. An "A" is not easily come by in my courses and my discussions have never been accused of being "lively" or "exciting," but they have been described as "thought provoking." My approach requires that I take a leading role in the discussion. The questions I pose are usually difficult because they require some degree of synthesis or analysis of material from either the reading or an earlier lecture. While any student response usually wins some positive comment from me, if it contains the kernel of an original or interesting idea I will usually put pressure on the student to develop or defend the idea further. The subsequent two- or three-minute dialogue is sometimes an excruciating experience for students, but the results are often a gem of some value and students at first are relieved and then gratifyingly impressed that they were more intelligent than they had thought. This process, repeated in classes and reinforced in the setting of paper topics, leads students not only to increased self-confidence in their ability to deal with problems, but also to a greater awareness of the distinctive nature of their own approaches.

A short while ago, I had a letter from a sophomore who had been in several of my courses. He was being forced to transfer to another college. In leaving Ripon, he said he knew that he still had a lot to learn, but he now had the confidence he could do so. While I have won more than my share of teaching prizes, it is the letters of this sort in which students recognize their ability to take control of their own education that I have taken as true the measure of my own teaching effectiveness. If indeed the education of new generations of self-directed and self-confident leaders is the particular province of liberal arts colleges, it seems to me that the most effective teaching in such institutions must be student-oriented.

Peer Interaction Boosts Science Learning[1]

F. S. Chew (Biology)
Tufts University

College science requires facts, conceptualization, and critical thinking

Scientific inquiry challenges factual knowledge and conceptual understanding, both of which are required for the successful practice of science[2] and the critical thinking needed for general scientific literacy by non-scientists and scientists alike.

College-level science courses require that students (a) digest and sort large amounts of factual information, much of which is continually recontextualized or replaced by newer findings; (b) simultaneously assimilate current conceptual models; and (c) learn academic skills needed to manipulate information and concepts. In addition, students have feelings (knowingly or not, willingly or not) about their abilities, science tasks, and classroom situations. Our challenge as educators is to help students internalize cognitive skills needed for science, while also assisting them as they deal with emotional issues that can promote or deter persistence.[3] This paper reviews some classroom methods I have implemented to address both cognitive and affective issues.[4]

Peer interaction is a norm in scientific research

Most of the modern scientific world works collaboratively. Collaboration's prevalence testifies to the effectiveness of working together where problems are complex. Even where scientists do not specifically collaborate, assistance from colleagues is widely acknowledged; but collaboration and acknowledgment—useful and widespread practices in scientific research—are rarely used to teach science. Further, although various groupwork methods have been implemented in schools, college teaching has rarely incorporated collaborative formats.

Peer interaction significantly enhances science achievement, both for younger pupils[5] and at the college level.[6] While peer interaction is often not best for learning rote or mechanical tasks (e.g., memorization of terms, procedures, formulae), appropriate peer collaboration significantly improves participants' achievement in conceptualization[7] and manipulation of complex problems, which constitutes much college level science.

I have implemented methods modelled on the interaction of colleagues whose contributions are acknowledged, but who do not actually work together. Although I also assign collaborative projects, I focus here on the "acknowledgement" model because products are graded individually. Given our institutional preoccupation with individual evaluation [at all levels from freshman courses to dealing with jointly authored work in professorial tenure cases], this model embodies a more appropriate use of peer assistance than pure collaboration. Students take substantial individual responsibility for their own achievement levels, but peer interactions enhance their achievement by providing opportunities for reflection, assessment, informational feedback, and support.

Classroom example 1: Information overload

Lecturing is an efficient mode for communicating lots of information to lots of listeners within a relatively short time-span. However, compared with other oral modes (for example one-to-one conversation), lecture formats deprive listeners of the time for reflection needed to internalize the material.

On the other hand, student dyads address the questions "What have I just heard? What makes sense? What's one question I have?" In pairs, students take sequential turns to answer these questions for a minute while the other pays attention and gives non-verbal encouragement. The session is monitored by the instructor, who also calls out "time to switch" after one minute has elapsed, and "that's time" after two minutes. Students ask more thoughtful questions following such pauses for cognitive processing, and quickly realize if they have missed important information. This method is similar to the "one-minute paper"[8] because both methods use cognitive processing via writing or talking. The one-minute paper requires less time and promotes writing practice, but because talking is faster than writing, dyad participants process more information per unit time.

Classroom example 2: Focusing attention

Short dyads assist students to "wake up" in an eight o'clock class. Students take 2-minute turns to consider the question "How are things going for me right now?" I encourage them to stretch, yawn and giggle during dyad time. I observe that students pay better attention, and tardiness declines. To focus attention on a specific topic, such as island biogeography, I ask dyads to consider questions like "What do I know about islands? What associations do I have with islands?"

I may use student responses as a springboard for my lecture. A lecture on the genetics of cereal grasses may be prefaced by a dyad on "What do I think of when I hear the word 'grass'?" These dyads offer opportunity to reflect on knowledge and feelings and help students place new information in the context of what they already know.

Classroom example 3: Solving problems and critical thinking

Dyads can also be used for more complex tasks if one allows more time per turn. Here, students use each others' assistance to work on individual assignments, much as an individual scientist's work or manuscript is enhanced by consultation with another scientist whose contribution is acknowledged.

The reviewing scientist is not usually more expert in the topic than the writer; both writer and reviewer are often explorers of little-known territory.

Students use these interactions to think critically and write about unresolved scientific and policy issues. They must decide (a) what subject to write about; (b) how to construct their arguments; (c) how to present those arguments persuasively; and (d) what positive alternatives to propose to respond to criticisms.

Students use peer interactions extensively for support during the process of writing and revising successive drafts. Interactions focus on assessing one's own thinking and writing, with the attention and encouragement (but not advice) of a peer. Students report that peer encouragement keeps them focused on the task and enables them to deal constructively with feelings. Students use dyads to recognize when they are missing information, and when their thinking is strongly influenced by values and non-scientific agenda. Awareness of and distinction between reactions and thinking improves classroom discussion and enables students to construct arguments more persuasively.

Interactions create a learning community of peers

If used regularly, dyads socialize the classroom into a learning community. Students get acquainted with each other as peers. Formation of a learning community among course members shifts emphasis from the teacher to students. This shift facilitates students seeing each other as resources, and seeing their job as doing and assessing their own work, rather than (merely) figuring out what the instructor wants.

Within a few dyad sessions, students discover whether they are confused because they are missing important information; distracted by an immediate need such as hunger; or "daydreaming" because they are preoccupied with feelings about something. While remedies for the first two situations are relatively simple, the third is less easily dealt with in a classroom context. As long as a student's attention is occupied by feelings, cognitive processes will be blocked.[9] Access to cognitive functions can be restored by releasing or discharging the stored emotional tension through the expressive aspect of affect[10]—the physical laughing, yawning, sweating, shaking and crying that we do when we feel embarrassed, scared or sad. This non-verbal expression of feelings represents the physical manifestation of our natural ability to rid ourselves of emotional distress.[11] Rules are (a) equal time per student; (b) giggling, yawning, and other spontaneous behavior is fine; (c) no interruption or advice; (d) confidentiality.

After an opportunity to acknowledge and discharge feelings, students find they can better focus their attention on a cognitive task.[12]

Peer dyads promote autonomy in learning by providing students with opportunities to construct their own conceptual frameworks and to reflect on their progress. These formats also promote equality by structurally ensuring each peer has uninterrupted time to think or feel. Shy or less verbal students often realize they have something to say if they don't have to talk immediately. More assertive students learn to be succinct and to listen.

Students learn collaborative skills in the classroom

As emphasized by practitioners of many groupwork models, students must learn social skills in order to work together effectively. By the time they get to college, students have spent too many years working in isolation to work together without guidance. Instruction in collaborative skills consists principally of peers learning to listen attentively and confidentially to each other—without interruption, advice, or judgment— to provide a space to think out loud. I give student dyads the in-class assignment of taking turns listening silently for one minute and of being listened to for one minute without verbal feedback. It's actually a difficult task on both ends because we are socialized to give and receive immediate feedback in conversational interactions. But the point of taking turns is to do our own thinking aloud with an approving audience and without interruption, advice, or judgment, so we have the opportunity to really do our own thinking and to realize we have feelings.[13]

For more extended applications such as peer editing, there are helpful ways for peers to give feedback.[14] For example, in 20-minute turns, issues can be raised such as personal concerns (e.g., "I got confused here." "I wasn't sure where you were going with this thought.") or as questions (e.g., "Do you have a specific audience in mind?" "Would your audience benefit from an example?")

Peer interaction helps learners take charge of their own education

Implementation of these peer interactions reduces my lecture time 10-15%. However, students pay better attention and ask better questions, so I repeat myself less frequently. I find that student problem-solving, papers, and take-home exams are more thoughtful and well-written as a result of the interactions. Further, because students acknowledge each other's assistance, they are keenly aware of plagiarism. Best, students report a sense of autonomy, confidence, and awareness in their thinking and writing processes that goes well beyond my courses. Many say that they have improved confidence in their own abilities to tackle problems. Others report improved social skills, particularly in getting to know people who are quite different from themselves. Women in particular report they become more assertive.

Part of educating young scientists involves gradually giving them increased responsibility for figuring things out, whether the task involves simple procedures, complex problem solving, interpreting technical information, or finding outside expert help for one's project. The major challenge for me (as a teacher with substantial research and consulting responsibilities, as well as teaching duties) is to enable students to internalize cognitive skills in a supportive context that doesn't focus primarily on "expert" advice from me.[15]

When students finish their degrees they are suddenly expected (for doctoral level students) to oversee their own major projects, write their own grants, and negotiate their own collaborative arrangements. Because these undergraduate collaborative formats enable students to think productively without "expert" company, students gradually realize they can tackle problems with minimum expert help. To the extent that higher education focuses science education on the "expert" teacher, we seriously mislead students about the actual practice of science and complex problem solving. Autonomy and confidence, as well as the ability to listen to others, are critical in educating potential scientists and others who can successfully tackle the substantial global problems we currently face.

Ironically, giving up certain kinds of control and being willing to live with the appearance of chaos has generated a richness and a degree of independence, cooperation, affection, and creativity that I wouldn't have imagined. It has been exhilarating.

Notes

1. G. M. Puttick, a research biologist and educator at Technical Education Research Center, 2067 Massachusetts Ave., Cambridge, MA 02140, has co-developed and co-led our collaborative learning workshops and courses in academic and multicultural contexts since 1988. Jane Hill Detenber has helped me to think and write since 1984. E.D. va der Reijden, L. Flanagan, and G.M. Puttick read the manuscript. The Mary Ingraham Bunting Institute, Radcliffe College, provided encouragement to explore these ideas. The H. Dudley Wright Foundation supported some recent developments.

2. Empirical observations enhance construction of conceptual models; models enhance the ability to put data into patterns. See R.E. Cook (1977). Raymond Lindeman and the trophic-dynamic concept in ecology. *Science* 198:22-26; S. Toulmin and J. Goodfield (1965). *The Discovery of Time.* Chicago: Univ. of Chicago Press, 125ff.

3. For example, Ruskai, M.B., (1991). Comment: Are there innate cognitive gender differences? Some comments on the evidence in response to a letter from M. Levin. *American Journal of Physics* 59, 11-14.

4. I have implemented these methods in several intermediate courses with a heterogeneous mixture of undergraduates from biology and graduate students from

several departments. I also teach an undergraduate course in leadership and multicultural awareness that makes extensive use of these methods for addressing diversity issues.

5. For review, see R.E. Slavin, editor (1990). *Cooperative Learning, theory, research and practice.* Englewood Cliffs, NJ: Prentice-Hall; and Sharan, S., editor (1990). *Cooperative Learning, theory and research.* New York: Praeger.

6. Light, R.J. (1990, 1991). The Harvard Assessment Seminars. Cambridge, MA: Harvard University.

7. Damon, W. and Phelps, E. (1989). Critical distinctions among three approaches to peer education. *International Journal of Educational Research* 13, 9-19; Phelps, E. and Damon, W. (1989). Problem solving with equals: peer collaboration as a context for learning mathematics and spatial concepts. *Journal of Educational Psychology. 81,* 639-646.

8. I have also implemented writing methods developed and taught at the Bard College Institute for Writing and Thinking along with these collaborative methods that emphasize talking. My students use writing when working alone but have found these talking formats more productive for cognitive processing, perhaps because there is more peer support.

9. Piaget, J. (1981). *Intelligence and affectivity: their relationship during child development.* Palo Alto, CA: Annual Reviews.

10. Ibid.

11. Jackins, H. (1964). *The human side of human beings.* Seattle, WA: Rational Island Press.

12. J. H. Detenber, a fifth grade teacher and A. Vhlahakis, a high school teacher, have adapted the "wake-up" exercise for non-dyad use in their classrooms in the morning or after lunch. Detenber instructs students to fake yawns and raise their hands when real yawns come, and when everyone's hands are up [usually two minutes], the exercise is over; Vhlahakis gives students two minutes to "yawn and

stretch," but they are not to talk or otherwise make much noise. Both report students' attention to cognitive tasks improves dramatically.

13. The difference between normal conversational interactions and really listening or being listened to needs to be experienced. Methods similar to these have been described as constructivist listening, see J. Weissglass (1990). Constructivist listening for empowerment and change. *Education Forum* 54, 352-370. To demonstrate the difference, I use the following short exercise: (i) one-minute fake listening and one minute trying to talk to a fake listener [during this exercise, the listener makes obvious attempts to ignore the talker, who tries to think aloud about a question such as "What's something I do well as a student/teacher that many of my peers don't know about?"]; (ii) one minute real listening and one minute thinking aloud with a real listener [during this exercise, listeners maintain eye contact, give non-verbal encouragement such as nodding the head, etc.]. If students observe most conversations, they discover that most participants aren't really listening. Each is waiting for a chance to contribute, and the urge to do so often results in interruptions at intervals of less than one minute. Satisfying conversations are those where participants really do listen to each other. Confidentiality is important to promote safety, and the injunction against interruption or advice gives the talker space to think about her or his own agenda; further, there are plenty of non-dyad times for students to give each other feedback, advice, etc., and dyads are a time for students to reflect without interruption. The approving listener approves of the talker's effort to think, even if the talker takes a temporary wrong turn in her/his reasoning. We all gain satisfaction and confidence from working through our confusions without being given the "correct" answer.

14. Peer editing and feedback do not substitute for feedback from an instructor, but instructors also are not sole proprietors of useful feedback.

15. For discussion of long term motivational effects, see A. Kohn (1991). Group grade grubbing versus cooperative

learning.; R.E. Slavin (1991). Group rewards make group-work work, response to Kohn; and A. Kohn (1991). Don't spoil the promise of cooperative learning, response to Slavin. *Educational Leadership*, Feb., 83–94.

About the Contributors

Mary Ball is a member of the Department of Biology at Carson-Newman College, Jefferson City, Tennessee 37760. She received her B.S. degree in mathematics from Trinity University in San Antonio and both her M.S. and Ph.D. degrees in genetics from Texas A & M. Prior to coming to Carson-Newman, Prof. Ball was on the faculty at Auburn University. She taught high school mathematics before earning her master's degree. Her current scholarly interests include biological monitoring of stream quality, methods of promoting scientific literacy, environmental education, and the "science-technology-society" approach to teaching science. In 1990 she was recognized for outstanding teaching in Appalachia by the Faculty Scholars Program of the Graduate School of the University of Kentucky.

Donna Bauerly is a member of the Department of English at Loras College in Dubuque, Iowa 52001. She received her B.A. degree from Briar Cliff College and both her Master's and Ph.D. from Marquette University. Before coming to Loras she was an NDEA Fellow-Teacher at Marquette and an English teacher in junior high and high school. She has made presentations and published regarding a wide cross-section of topics in literature including reading and teaching poetry in secondary education. She has taught at-risk children and adolescents in settings other than schools and colleges.

Joseph Buckley is a member of the Department of Philosophy at John Carroll University, University Heights, Ohio 44118. He received his B.A. from Providence College, and his M.A. and Ph.D. from Notre Dame. He has specialized in logic and metaphysics and has published articles on "... the concept of work," problem solving and critical thinking as well as other topics. For several years he served as the Director of the Honors Program at John Carroll.

Frances Chew is a member of the Department of Biology at Tufts University in Medford, Massachusetts 02155. She received her A.B. degree from Stanford and her Ph.D. from Yale. She has been a prolific scholar for over fifteen years publishing and presenting papers in entomology and other areas. Since 1981 she has been a member of the Affiliated Faculty of the Department of Urban and Environmental Policy at Tufts and since 1991 she has served as a visiting lecturer in the Experimental College of the Tufts Department of Education. In the latter role she is developed and currently teaches a course "Taking Initiative" which addresses issues of prejudice reduction, multiculturalism, and leadership for undergraduates. She also has developed and teaches a course for middle and secondary teachers and education students called "Collaborative Learning."

Lucy Cromwell is a member of the Department of English at Alverno College, Milwaukee, Wisconsin 53215. She received both her B.A. and M.A. degrees from the University of Denver and her Ph.D. from the University of Wisconsin-Milwaukee. While at Alverno she has been an active scholar in her particular field and also in interdisciplinary efforts. For example, she has designed an orientation program for new faculty, directed a FIPSE grant to develop networks of faculty studying critical thinking, and made presentations to educational groups regarding critical thinking, assessment, and values.

Timothy Garner is a member of the Department of Sociology at Franklin College, Franklin, Indiana 46131. He received his B.A. from Franklin and both his A.M. and Ph.D. from the University of Illinois at Urbana-Champaign. He taught at the University of Illinois and Sterling College before returning to Franklin. His scholarly interests have included social psychology, popular culture, and social problems. His doctoral dissertation examined the effects of videogaming. Prof. Garner was the first Franklin College recipient of the Sears Foundation and Council for Independent Higher Education Award for Teaching Excellence and Campus Leadership.

Janet Griffin is on the faculty of the Department of History at Our Lady of the Lake University, San Antonio, Texas 78207-4666. She received her B.S. degree there before earning both the M.A. and Ph.D. from St. Louis University. Prior to returning to her alma mater Sr. Griffin taught in junior high schools and other colleges in the southwest. Her scholarly interests in recent years have centered on "feminism of women religious" a topic about which she has written a number of articles and given several presentations. She has received a Teaching Excellence Award and recognition as the Outstanding Faculty Member of the Year since returning to Our Lady of the Lake.

Bruce Griffith is a member of the Department of History at Catawba College in Salisbury, North Carolina 28144. He received his B.A. degree from Catawba and both his M.A. and Ph.D. degrees from the University of North Carolina-Chapel Hill. In addition to his scholarly interest in western and world history, Prof. Griffith has participated in several interdisciplinary activities: He has team-taught "Earth Management," made presentations regarding Catawba's freshman year experience, and been author and project director of a National Endowment for the Humanities Grant entitled "Humanities Centered Coherence in General Education" at Catawba College. Also, he has received the Swink Award for Outstanding Classroom Teaching.

Rose Marie Hurrell, a psychologist, is on the faculty of the College of New Rochelle in New Rochelle, New York 10801. She received her B.A. from Lehman College of the City University of New York and both M.A. and Ph.D. degrees from Fordham University. In addition to her faculty work she has consulted in various areas and has published and made presentations regarding alcohol abuse, sexuality, decision-making in families, spirituality, and stress. She has been an active participant in regional psychological associations as well as college boards and committees.

Thomas Kasulis was nominated and selected to write for this monograph while he was on the faculty of Northland College in Ashland, Wisconsin, as Professor of Philosophy and Religion. Since then he has moved to Ohio State University where he is on the faculty of Comparative Studies in Humanities, Philosophy & Religion. He received B.A., M. Phil., and Ph.D. degrees from Yale and a M.A. from the University of Hawaii. Prof. Kasulis's academic focus has centered on Asian and comparative religions with a special interest in Japan. He has published and lectured widely in Japan and the United States.

Patricia O'Connell Killen is a member of the Department of Religion at Pacific Lutheran University in Tacoma, Washington 98447. She received her B.A. from Gonzaga University and both her M.A. and Ph. D. degrees from Stanford. Her scholarly interests include social theory and theology of church and community. She has published and presented widely in these areas. Prof. Killen also has contributed to theological education, the training of mentors for the ministry, and programs of nontraditional theological education. Her collaboration with Dennis Martin is the only co-authored article for this volume.

Harvey Klevar is presently Professor of Anthropology at Luther College in Decorah, Iowa 52101. He also has background and experience as a faculty member in English at Luther and elsewhere. Prof. Klevar earned his B.A. from the University of St. Thomas in Houston, Texas, and both his M.A. and Ph.D. from the University of Minnesota. His scholarly work has combined literature and anthropology at several points. He has a long-standing interest in family, the American South, and Erskine Caldwell.

Dennis Martin is a member of the English Department at Pacific Lutheran University in Tacoma, Washington 98447. He received a B.S. from Edinboro State College, an M.A. from Purdue, and a Ph.D. from UCLA. He specializes in modern American literature especially as it involves the arts, sciences, and history. He has worked on interdisciplinary projects involving enlightenment philosophies, the French revolution, Darwinian biology, and various topics in music and art. Prof. Martin has authored questions for the Graduate Record Exam in Literature, and he has served as a reviewer for the National Teacher's Exam. His collaboration with Prof. Killen is the only co-authored article for this volume.

Marcia Ann McDonald is a member of the Department of Literature and Language at Belmont University in Nashville, Tennessee 37212. She earned her B.A. from Stetson University and both her M.A. and Ph.D. from Vanderbilt. In addition to her scholarly interests in English, many of which have involved Shakespeare, Prof. McDonald has written and lectured about teaching. She received the Chaney Distinguished Professor Award from Belmont in 1988 and gave the Distinguished Humanities Lecture there in 1991.

Robert McJimsey is Professor of History at Colorado College in Colorado Springs, Colorado 80903. He received his B.A. from Grinnell College and both his M.A. and Ph.D. from the University of Wisconsin. Prior to coming to Colorado Prof. McJimsey taught at Oberlin College, Ohio Wesleyan University, and Iowa State University. He has had a long interest in English history and has travelled and studied in the United Kingdom several times. His teaching has included a number of interdisciplinary courses which address issues of revolution, freedom, and authority, among others.

John Oppelt is a member of the Mathematics and Computer Science Department at Bellarmine College in Louisville, Kentucky 40205. He has held the Capitol Holding Chair of Mathematics since 1989. Prof. Oppelt earned his B.A. from Loyola College in Baltimore and both his M.S. and Ph.D. degrees from Notre Dame. He has written and spoken widely and received grants regarding middle and high school teaching. He has spent many years as a college administrator as well as teacher. He was a recipient of the Greater Louisville Council Award of Teaching Excellence in 1990.

David Oswald is a faculty member in the Department of Communications and Theatre Arts at Cardinal Stritch College, in Milwaukee, Wisconsin 53217. He received both his B.A. and M.A. degrees from Michigan State University. In addition to directing over sixty-five theatre productions in community, educational, and semi-professional settings, Prof. Oswald has been an active program developer and participant in Wisconsin professional theatre and theatre education organizations. He received the Sears-Roebuck Foundation Award for Teaching Excellence and Academic Leadership for 1989-90.

Daniel Schroeder is Professor of Physics and Astronomy at Beloit College in Beloit, Wisconsin 53511. After earning his B.S. at Beloit, he went on to the University of Wisconsin in Madison where he completed a Ph.D. program. He has been an active scholar for years especially in the area of spectroscopy. He is a member of the National Aeronautics and Space Administration team that developed the Hubble Space Telescope. Prof. Schroeder has won the Teacher of the Year award for Beloit College faculty members in three different decades.

Jesse Scott is a member of the History department at Newberry College, Newberry, South Carolina 29108. He received his B.A. and M.A. degrees from Clemson University and his Ph.D. from the University of South Carolina. In addition to an active scholarly life regarding his specialty in European history, Prof. Scott has maintained an intense interest in teaching. He has participated in conferences regarding assessment, science education, and humanities teaching. He received the Sears Roebuck Foundation Award for "Teaching Excellence and Campus Leadership" presented at the Founders Day Convocation held in 1990 at Newberry.

Laura Winters is a member of the English department at the College of St. Elizabeth, Convent Station, New Jersey 07961. She received B.A., M.Phil., and Ph.D. degrees from Drew University and an M.A. from Rutgers. She has been an active scholar during her academic career continuing an early interest in Willa Cather. Prof. Winters has studied Ms. Cather and other writers regarding "space" and gender. Prof. Winters has also contributed to reflection on teaching in articles such as "Implicit and Explicit Values in the Graduate Classroom."

William Wooley is Professor of History and Helen Swift Neilson Professor of Cultural Studies at Ripon College in Ripon, Wisconsin 54971. He earned his B.A. from Dartmouth College and both M.A. and Ph.D. degrees from Indiana University. Over the years he has published several articles and presented papers regarding warfare with a special interest in George S. Patton. Prof. Wooley has repeatedly received honors for teaching success at Ripon winning the Senior Class Teaching Award six times from 1971 to 1991 and the Severy Teaching Award four times.